A

God-filled

Nobody

John Beaumont

ISBN 0–476–00444–6

Printed by Outreach Press,

Christchurch, New Zealand

Published by Renewal Ministries

P.O. Box 186, Rangiora, New Zealand

Contents

A God-filled Nobody

FOREWORD

I HAVE JUST FINISHED INDULGING IN A HUGE feast. The table was groaning with goodies, and I sampled everything! Instead of feeling overfed and lethargic, however, I feel greatly invigorated. In fact, I feel slimmed-down for action. I was running a race, and I know I am all the more ready to continue!

… These are the best words I can find to describe my experience of reading this new book by John Beaumont!

Over the twenty years I have known John, any recollections-of-the-past he has mentioned, in preaching or in conversation, have always been something of a treat. His anecdotes never failed to be worth listening to: amusing, or intriguing—and yet invariably nourishing. They fed our spirits. They strengthened our responsiveness to the Lord Jesus.

Now, in these "memoirs" John has, as it were, provided us with a banquet—a table laden with his recollections from many different parts of the world. I have feasted at this table with great pleasure, and I know that I am stronger, and spiritually fitter, as a result.

A God-filled Nobody

There is no doubt whatsoever, in my mind, that many Christian people, across the globe, are going to be richly blessed as they read the pages ahead.

I would like to mention three truths of which I have become much more sure, as a result of reading this book. I am not saying that God will necessarily underline exactly the same principles in every reader's heart. I merely want to emphasise that John's reminiscences seem to highlight priceless biblical truths.

The first is: "Those who are led by the Spirit of God are the sons of God." It is clear throughout the book that John always made a determined practice of listening-to-the-Spirit before replying or reacting in any situation. He consciously set aside the expectations of those involved, or his own opinions based on previous experience, and listened for the Spirit's voice. Over and over again, there was a remarkable outcome. (You will find numerous examples in what John has written.) Most of us pay lip-service to this principle, of course—but very few of us really put it into practice. I think this book will help us to deeply desire to be "led by the Spirit".

The second principle which came across power-fully to me was this: "Speak the truth in love". John was always willing to speak the truth, even if it was going to be very hard for the hearer to take. However, each time he first-of-all sought the Spirit's guidance on how the truth spoken could become up-build-ing in the person's life. Speaking-the-truth-in-love doesn't mean presenting the truth in a palatable way. (Sugaring the pill, which is what most of us try to do!) It means presenting the truth in a productive way.

Lastly, I want to mention the unusual biblical phrase "married to another—even to Him who is raised from the dead". (Romans 7:4. A.V.) John's happy marriage to Mary shines through these pages—but so does this other marriage of his! (Isn't it wonderful that the love-relationship with one's spouse, and the love-relationship with Jesus, are not mutually exclusive. In fact, we learn lessons about each partnership from the other partnership.) Whether we are mar-ried or single, however, I am convinced that reading this book will help us all understand more clearly what the Authorized Version meant when it said we should be "married to another...that we might bear fruit to God".

Well! You are at the starting-end of the table. I have tried to give you a glimpse of some of the good things that lie ahead. I know that, in the end, your plate may carry a different selection to mine. But I genuinely believe you will step out, after you have finished, renewed and refreshed, and better prepared than ever to run the race that is set before you.

Stan Firth

INTRODUCTION

THIS IS AN ATTEMPT TO SHARE SOME OF life's experiences and lessons in such a way that it becomes solely a testimony to the grace of God. The credit is all His for anything worthwhile coming out of my life. On the other hand, the blame for every flaw, fault and failure is mine alone. Over the years I have asked Father to allow me to be, and remain, a hidden man, even though frequently in the public eye, only aspiring to be a God filled nobody.

Years ago I dreamed that I saw people gathered for a memorial service at the end of my earthly life. It was being held in a community hall rather than in a church building.

As everyone became quiet just before the start, a man I knew rushed in and asked, "Where is he?" No one answered, and so he asked the same question louder and louder. In moments everyone was exclaiming as if it were a chant, "John is not here. John is not here!"

All eyes turned to a friend—not a minister—who slowly walked forward and said, "John is not here, he is with the Lord. We are here to celebrate the grace of God in John's life."

I joked with one or two that it wasn't surprising that the Christian man who rushed in, and who will remain nameless, asked that question. I often felt that he didn't know where I was even when we were together!

Possibly the first time I shared at any length about the grace of God was in a meeting in Kingston, New York. One of the elders there, Dale Rumble, told me afterwards that for them such a topic had extra significance. They had noted over the years that whenever the Lord intended taking them into new realms of Christian living and serving, it had been preceded by a heightened emphasis on the grace of God.

To me the grace of God is the active expression of all that He is in His intrinsic nature, being extended to a totally unworthy person such as I am. This is in order that we may live a Christ-honouring life as we walk in the fullness of God's purpose and provision for them.

To put it a little differently, *divine grace is all that God is, made available for all that I lack, to enable me to be all that He chooses.*

I am most grateful to the Holy Spirit who not only stirred me to write this book, but who has also been my Encourager throughout. My wife Mary has been very supportive as we have shared memories together and discussed the best way to express them. David and Nina Rice have willingly undertaken the task of editing and proof reading. This has been most helpful and is deeply appreciated. At the end of that process I received this letter:

"At a personal level may I say that this has been a very enjoyable and stimulating exercise. The more I read the manuscript the more absorbing it becomes. I do think it is worthy of wide distribution in whatever form seems best to you.

"I would also like to put on record the enormous impact that your life has had on me. I was initially hugely helped by the clarity of the word of the Lord that you spoke in Donegal. Subsequently the biggest impact that your life has had on me was in the way you responded to the Spirit, usually at great cost, when you were staying with us during Mary's illness, and when we were in Sweden together.

"At that time I learned to stand up in the strength

of the Lord and not be afraid of the consequences of obedience. Such things cannot be taught, they must be caught. By the overflow of the grace of the Lord in your life, I caught some things which totally changed and re-formed me and continue to do so. I will always be grateful to Jesus for those experiences as well as the many other evidences of His grace in our fellowship through the years.

Bless Jesus for His faithfulness, grace and love. David."

In the Scriptures, the Apostle Paul didn't simply follow the custom of his people in wishing others, "Peace." His greeting was always, "Grace and peace." I greet you thus today. May you, who-ever you are, '*be blessed in the heavenly realms with every spiritual blessing in Christ*,' by the grace of God alone.

Part 1

Childhood and Youth

A God-filled Nobody

Childhood and Youth

T HERE WELL MAY BE NO ASPECT OF LIFE where a person's memory is as selective and subjective, as in their early years. We probably all know of times when in adulthood a sibling has spoken of a childhood event, only to hear something quite different from our own recollection of it. Moreover, we have scant understanding of what has been happening in the mind and heart of anyone else, even though we may clearly recall our own fears, phobias, frustrations, hurts, desires, aspirations and struggles. I shall try to share only what I believe has bearing on this attempt to focus on the grace of God in my life.

My shyness as a youngster did not come from the fact that we were very poor. That applied to many others. Only later on did I recognise how much shame and fear had affected me. Without wanting to dwell on it at all, I must mention that I was very afraid of my dad and his erratic and sometimes violent behaviour. I was deeply ashamed of the kind of man he was. I will only mention that a family member who knew the truth from personal sad experience, made this statement to me in later years: "If those things happened today he would be given a hefty prison sentence."

For the record, I was born in Tauranga, New Zealand, on the thirteenth of December 1932, the third of five children.

My mother's sensitive reliance on her Lord, and her kindness and love, were a place of refuge and a repeated source of encouragement to us all. She once told me of an occasion when I was a baby. She was wheeling me in a pram along a dusty country road, making her way, I think, to get a few things from a little general store. Along the road came some cattle.

Mother was terrified of them even though she lived in a country area. She simply could not help it, she just had to rush to the roadside fence, climb through it and leave me there! Apparently a bull came up to the pram, showed interest in it, putting his head right inside the hood. However, after a short while the cattle moved on, mother climbed back through the fence, and I was none the worse for wear!

In a General Store you could buy just about anything, as the name implies. Everything was so different then. Here are a few examples: Flour and sugar came in quite large bags which purchasers later washed and used for making everything from aprons to floor mats. Biscuits and other products were bought by the pound and placed in paper bags that came in various sizes. A pound of broken biscuits was a good cheap buy from a child's pocket money—if he got any! There was no such thing as a plastic bag. Plastic hadn't yet been invented! Candles and kerosene were often on shopping lists.

Quick frozen foods did not exist. If you wanted bacon the grocer sliced it with a gadget that held the bacon piece and sliced it with a rotating blade. Cheese was cut to order with a thin wire attached to a cheese board. Parcels were wrapped in brown paper that was drawn from a roll at the end of the counter. The parcel was tied with string, the storekeeper usually breaking it by twisting it around a finger and tugging. Sellotape didn't exist.

I began school at the Mangatapu Native School. That is what was printed in large lettering at the front of the school, although such a thing would be unacceptable today. Almost all the children were Maori. The three mile walk to school along country roads seemed an enormous distance.

A God-filled Nobody

I hadn't been at school long when we moved to Mount Maunganui to live, and so we went to the primary school there. When high school days began we had to take a half-hour ferry ride across to Tauranga and then travel by bus to the school.

When I left school at fifteen years of age I worked in several offices, including working at a bank for several years. During that time my parents' marriage came apart completely. My mother moved to Christchurch with Ivy and Bruce, her youngest children. After some time I followed them, little realising the significance of the move.

As a child I had opened up my heart to the Saviour, been involved in Sunday School and church life, and attended Bible Class activities. I had childhood fantasies of myself as a missionary living in a cave in some exotic foreign land. In fact, though nobody knew of it, there were times when I walked across the paddocks to school I would pause, if nobody was in sight, and proclaim the gospel to open space.

In Christchurch I became deeply involved with the Youth for Christ movement whose director was the much-loved Malcolm Miles. While I was still in Tauranga I stepped into an older brother's shoes when he had been asked to testify at YFC there. Trouble was, my shyness took over and I cried right there on the platform. That seems shameful to a teenager.

Youth for Christ

THOSE YOUTH FOR CHRIST DAYS WERE great times for many of us, who still thank God for His grace in our own lives then as well as for the wonders He accomplished among us. I loved the youth rallies, beach gatherings, open-air meetings, prayer sessions, youth camps and so on. To be with other young people whose hearts' desires were akin to mine was very precious. We were probably at the cutting edge of what God was doing in our city at that time.

Billy Graham came into prominence in those days. He was the Vice President of Youth For Christ International, whose motto was "Geared to the times, anchored to the Rock." At least in Christchurch, YFC was very different then from what it is now. We were more a general evangelistic agency, but still focused on youth. One month of the year we had an early prayer meeting each morning before anyone went to work. Not only were there times of prayer prior to rallies, but often right through them. From time to time there was a day of prayer, and for quite some time we had a night of prayer once a month.

For two years Jim Shortcliffe and I travelled around the South Island conducting children's missions. In the realm of walking with Christ, involvement in this work became a steep learning curve for me. During that time I feasted on the writings of Commissioner Brengle, Ruth Paxon and the like. I also read all the sermons preached years before in Nelson by the inimitable Irish preacher, Billy Nicholson. The Nelson newspaper had printed them in full.

I began to see Zechariah 4:6 as the theme for my life: "*Not by might nor by power, but by my Spirit says the Lord of Hosts.*" Later in paraphrase form it became for me "*Not by human strength or ability, nor by the supportive power of an army of men, but by my Spirit says the Lord of heaven's armies.*"

There was a time, while Jim and I were travelling, that I became very burdened about inconsistencies in my life. I could tell young people that when we yielded our lives to Christ we become a whole new creation in Him, but I knew that at times I had inner attitudes that were not right. Because there is level ground at the Cross I could not hide behind an inferiority complex.

For some days I spent hours and hours crying out to God for help. I read and re-read the Acts of the Apostles. I knew that early Christians must have found a solution to my kind of problem. At last this promise dawned on me: "I will pour out my Spirit on all flesh." I saw that 'all' must be able to include even a 'nobody' like me, and somehow I appropriated its reality that day. What Ruth Paxon described as, "Life on a higher plane" now made sense, and I believe came to be more real in me.

After those two years, while living in Christchurch again, I would frequently go to the YFC office in Colombo Street. Signs had been put up stating, 'Africa, 75 millions untold' 'South America, 70 millions untold' and so on. There was a map of the world and flags had been placed across it indicating places where missionaries who had spoken at the rally were working.

Again and again I prayed earnestly, with those statistics and the world map in front of me. At this time I was deeply touched by Amy Carmichael's vision which will be printed at the end of what I write about India. Before too long these things combined to give me a deep burden for India. YFC arranged for me to go there for two years. At twenty-two years of age I was young and inexperienced, but I had a burning heart of love for my Lord and for the lost of earth.

A God-filled Nobody

Part 2

India

A God-filled Nobody

FLYING WAS VERY DIFFERENT IN 1954 from what it is today. The first segment of my journey to India was from Christchurch to Sydney, where I was transferred to a hotel for an overnight stay. The next morning we started out early with Darwin being the first stop for refuelling. From there we flew to Jakarta in Indonesia, and thence to Singapore.

That night the airline arranged for me to stay in the renowned Raffles Hotel. I didn't simply have a hotel room, but an entire suite—all provided by the airline. More than that, a domestic servant seemed to be stationed in the corridor right outside my door for the entire time I was there, eager to serve me in whatever way I might require. I did not need him! The dining room décor was magnificent and the meal outstanding. There were photos around showing people dining with a bearer [servant] standing behind each chair, but that night there was a waiter for every four or five people.

When I stepped outside the hotel to look around a little I was quickly approached and followed by a cycle-rickshaw rider who hounded me asking incessantly, "You want pretty lady?" and adding, "Me take you [to] pretty lady." It was so embarrassing that I quickly returned to my hotel rooms.

The next morning we flew on to Colombo in Ceylon—now Sri Lanka—and after a refuelling break for the plane and lunch break for the passengers, we set out on the last leg of the journey, to Bombay which is now named Mumbai.

The heat at each stop from Darwin on had been quite stifling. Here in Bombay I felt that I was walking into an oven. Gradually one grows accustomed to climate changes, although it was a repeated challenge to me during my two momentous years in India. In later years when asked how we adjusted to climate changes my reply would be that spiritual climate changes are harder to cope with. In that sense one may not travel far and yet seem to move from the tropics to the South Pole, or vice versa.

Early Impressions

INEVITABLY FIRST IMPRESSIONS FADE somewhat, especially since a span of about fifty years has elapsed since my going there, and yet some things stand out very clearly in my memory.

It took a while to understand why there was so much reddish stuff splattered on the footpaths, in doorways and on the bottoms of walls. Chewing betel nuts was very very common and those chewing simply spat out the red juice just about wherever they felt like it. On at least one occasion someone spat it on my clean white clothes, ruining them since it could not be removed. It seemed to be deliberate.

Carrying goods on heads never ceased to amaze me even after seeing it frequently in Africa in later years. In Bombay there were scores of men and women who carried a huge long load of tiffin boxes or billy-cans which I was told contained lunches for some of the thousands of workers who came into that large and teeming city each day. These carriers moved along, carrying their burdens, at a fast walk or steady jog.

A God-filled Nobody

One day I looked out of a window in the fifth floor apartment I stayed in with Joe and Bernice Weatherly. A heavy piano was being carried down the street in a most unusual way. It was on the heads of six men. Each one had a turban tied around his head and on top of that was a brick. The piano was on its back, resting on the six bricks.

Whatever was the secret of these men being able to carry that piano right on down the long street, around the corner and out of sight without stopping once? Why on earth were bricks added to its weight? It didn't take me long to discover the answer. After a little while, as all of the men kept in step, one of them stooped a fraction and removed the brick from his head. This way he could stay in place under the piano and yet have a rest from carrying it! He soon put his brick back again, taking up his share of the load. Before the piano went out of sight I saw another man have a rest in the same way. Smart, eh?

India seemed to have an endless number of beggars. There is a beggar caste, just as there is a caste of carpenters, a caste of thieves and so on. I was told on a number of occasions that beggars deliberately maim their children when they are young so that they can more deeply touch the pity of passers-by and invoke greater generosity. Some looked appallingly grotesque with uncovered wounds and sores crawling with hordes of flies. It was quite shocking to be grabbed around the ankles by an imploring beggar. Sadly, if you gave to one of them you were immediately overwhelmed by many others who kept following you and pleading endlessly.

Throughout the areas I travelled in India I was repeatedly shocked at how wealth and poverty were found side by side. On one occasion I was cycling with a missionary towards a large annual Hindu festival being held in a remote area where only meandering tracks existed and no car could go. We stopped to rest in a small village and were quickly invited to lunch in a nearby home.

It was a magnificent three-storied home, excellently furnished. The well-dressed host made us welcome and provided a lovely lunch. "Nice" you say? Yes, but with a big 'but'! Outside the home with its high walled boundaries we had seen villagers not only under-nourished, but actually starving and near death. To that wealthy home-owner they just seemed to be a nuisance for which he apologised!

A God-filled Nobody

You may be surprised that life seems very cheap in many countries, I suspect especially where there has been little or no Christian influence in past centuries. I recall walking along a Bombay street one day with an Indian friend. We were only a block away from the main business and shopping centre where tourists throng.

A dirty, ragged, skeletal man was lying curled up on the pavement. I asked my friend, "Is that man dead?" He replied, "If he isn't yet, he soon will be," and walked on. Each morning trucks would go around the streets picking up the dead and carrying them away for burning.

It was always surprising to see how white laundry became when one saw dhobi-wallahs [laundry people] dipping their washing in a stream that wasn't all that clean, bashing them on rocks, rinsing them in the stream, and laying them out to dry. I once took a photo of someone dipping kerosene tins into a canal so that they could take water back to their home for cooking and drinking. In the same photo, right there in the canal was someone bathing and someone washing a buffalo that was defecating.

In Bombay I was involved with many fine young people who were a challenge to me in their enthusiasm, warmth and delightful witness for Christ. I found similar folk like that across the country, but there were many times when I felt that local Christians and even missionaries had settled down to accepting things the way they were, rather than reaching out to the Lord for something better.

Was it Robert Kennedy who said, "*Some men see things the way they are, and ask 'Why?' I see things the way they should be, and ask 'Why not?'*" Being comfortable with the status quo is not a valid option for the Spirit-filled believer.

Spiritual lethargy and half-heartedness should be loathed, hated and feared! I have sometimes told people that there is one thing worse than being half-hearted, and that is to settle down and be comfortable in that state. Over many years now I have determined that by the grace of God I will maintain spiritual freshness all the days of my life. I love the statement in Hebrews chapter eleven that "All these were living by faith when they died."

John Tiebe from Canada was the Bombay Director of Youth for Christ. He once asked their young people to go on an outing of some kind, inviting me to go along as well. John told them that he would provide lunch for them all. If I recall aright there were thirty-five or forty of us.

There was considerable consternation when it was discovered that lunch to John did not mean a mid-day meal, but simply an afternoon bite. He asked some of us to 'chip in' to buy food for them all! Over the years we have known many occasions when something that seemed clear and obvious had a very different meaning to someone from a different country or culture.

Let me share one other thing about my early days in India. I went to a large city bank to open an ac-count so that I could deposit any bank drafts I might receive. Nobody had actually guaranteed me any financial support, but Malcolm Miles, the Youth For Christ Director in Christchurch had encouraged me to trust the Lord with them for my supply.

Anyway, when I filled in an application form to open an account I listed my occupation as 'Evan-gelist.' The bank officer immediately said, "I'm very sorry, but you can't open an account here." He commented that nobody there knew me.

At that moment, way back in the bank I saw a senior man I had met at a service the previous day. Somewhat reluctantly the man dealing with me went and spoke to him. When he came over he immediately said, "Of course he may open an account here." The first man pointed to my 'evangelist' answer and asked, "What about that?" The revealing reply was, "Oh he [that is, me,] is just being humble." I soon learned that in some Christian families—many of them only nominally Christian I suppose—any son that seemed no good for anything was dubbed an evangelist, even though he might never introduce one solitary person to his Lord and Saviour! It seemed to me that the same could just as well apply to the multitude of Hindu 'sadhus' or holy men too.

Rajnandgaon

AFTER THESE MANY YEARS IT WOULD BE difficult to share insights into my time in India in chronological order. Besides that, I want to hasten to share things I was privileged to experience in Rajnandgaon in Madhya Pradesh State. This village, of about 100,000 people I think, lies alongside the railway line roughly half way between Bombay and Calcutta.

It had been arranged that I would spend at least a month there initially, speaking in the local church for however many days I felt right. After that we would move the meetings out into a large flat topped tent or shamiana that could seat quite a few hundred people the way Indians sit squatted closely together on the ground. The tent came as baggage with me on the train from Bombay. It was intriguing to see local Christians off-load the tent with its huge bamboo poles on the opposite side from the station. They loaded it on a bullock cart and brought it to the Mission property by a circuitous route. This saved paying customs duty!

A week or two before I started out for Rajnandgaon a delightful and earnest young officer in the Indian navy, named David Appavoo, told me that he had decided to come with me. Later he would go to London to study at university there. When asked why he wanted to come his reply was, "Not to speak in meetings or take any public part whatsoever." Not as a singer either! His sole purpose would be to pray for me and to pray with me for God's blessing on the crusade.

I don't know how to relate time to praying. I do know however that this became a heart 'burden' to David and me to the extent that many nights one of us would wake up after only a few hours sleep to wait on the Lord. The other one would join in and together we would seek God for a deep, sovereign moving of the Holy Spirit in that area.

The local Christian who was interpreting for me had an interesting story. He had been private secretary to a maharajah until he contracted leprosy. He sought help at the Mission leprosarium. Not only was he healed of that dreaded disease, but he turned from Hinduism to personal faith in the Lord Jesus. When an Indian Christian doctor offered to straighten a twisted finger for him he declared that he wanted it left like that as a perpetual reminder to him of the lengths that God in his love had gone to bring him to salvation.

One day this interpreter asked David and me if we would like to go out to the leprosarium where he himself now worked. We learned that every morning at about five o'clock lepers gathered together to pray for revival in Rajnandgaon. I was touched by the thought that there was a unique selflessness in their praying.

They would always be outside of the city and therefore expected to gain nothing from an outpouring of the Holy Spirit. David and I cycled out there a number of times. It was all so touching! Here were lepers kneeling on a hard, cold concrete floor. Some of them only had stumps where feet or legs had been. Their chapel had window openings with neither glass nor shutters. We noticed pray-ers shivering in the early morning cold. India isn't always hot!

Revival

I T WAS PROBABLY OUR SECOND WEEKEND there when we decided in conjunction with the Mission leader that we would put up the tent that Saturday and have a church service in it on Sunday. Our thinking was that non-Christians had some strange ideas about how Christians worshipped in their forbidding looking brick church building. Loud speakers were fitted onto a cart and driven throughout the township. An announcement was made that the next morning everyone was invited to watch Christians at worship.

It was heart moving to see many locals sitting on the ground outside while several hundred Christians [nominally so, at least] sat in the tent which had no sides to it. Everything was open to the curious gaze of all who gathered outside.

This becomes a little embarrassing to me as I look back on my behaviour that day! Soon after I began speaking to the church I was halted by a strong conviction that I believed then, and still do now for that matter, was the persuasion of the Holy Spirit within me.

I have sometimes commented that it is easy to

obey God when we can see that the outcome will be acceptable to others and beneficial to ourselves. It is quite another matter, and a real test of discipleship, when we are aware that a very different result is likely! That is where our love and obedience to Christ is really tested.

The comparison is not ideal, but you may understand if I suggest that this is somewhat like situations in the business world that may be described as high risk, and yet be where the best results or profits may be found. Old time preachers sometimes told their hearers to 'go for broke'. Are some Christians too keen to take the safest, easiest and most orthodox and comfortable options in life where they are least likely to offend? You be the judge!

Anyway, I did it! I pointed to a man half way back on my right hand side and said, "Sir, God tells me you are sleeping with your neighbour's wife." He screamed and fell on his face. It seemed as though he was groaning, crying and praying all at once. Responding to his sincere repentance, God touched and changed his life that day. I had no idea at the time that he was a church elder!

As was the custom, all the women were sitting on the left-hand side. I pointed to one of them and called out, "Sister, do I have to declare what is hidden in your life?" She immediately cried out, "No, no, no," ran to the front and on her knees began to cry out asking God for mercy and forgiveness.

That day it seemed as though God was showing me the secret things in everyone's heart. More than that, it seemed as though they knew it was happening. Actually I needed to say little else as all across the congregation people were on their knees or on their faces. It seemed that the wholesome fear of God had come upon everyone in the tent, and on the onlookers outside as well. After some time cries of anguish and tears of repentance turned to exclamations of joy and praise.

The service went on for hours. Here and there someone would hurry out of the meeting to return later after trying to make amends for past wrongs. Nobody had suggested that course of action. We learned that some went to settle differences with neighbours they had treated poorly, some went to make restitution for things they had stolen, others went to be reconciled with another member of their family, and some went to the railway to pay for trips they had already taken. People like these came back wreathed in smiles of joy and relief, praising God.

It was all so amazing. At the moment I had begun speaking that morning the Mission leader's wife started running from their home where she was looking after their handicapped daughter so that their helpers could be in the service. She said later that her heart was pounding with one thought, "God has come, God has come!" Don't ask me to explain how the God who is here can come, as Augustine said, but it happens! Wonderfully!

When David and I had arrived at Rajnandgaon the Mission leader had told us two things, one sad and one strange. The sad thing was that there had not been one convert in that area for an entire generation. The strange thing was that he believed Satan was in control of their entire compound. The compound included not only the church building but also homes of missionaries and national workers, a school and a dormitory plus I don't know what else. That very day they saw their first convert for many a year.

Desiring Heaven's Best

THERE IS MUCH MORE TO WRITE ABOUT this, but let me quickly and strongly state that from that day on I was spoiled in the sense that no longer could I be satisfied with man's best. I had experienced sovereign God at work. We need, the church needs, and the world about us needs God's best—heaven's best. 'Playing church' and being religious is totally out of order. No doubt it always has been, but how much more so now in our day.

Hear me, fellow Christian. The idea that the more we do the quicker God's kingdom is established is a very common point of view, is it not? Earnest believers strive valiantly to do as much as possible for God. Add up all the gatherings, meetings, rallies, crusades, conferences, retreats, seminars, and like events in every church and every city and town throughout any of our countries and throughout the whole year. Include all of the preaching, teaching, prophesying and exhorting plus all of the singing, praising, worshipping, praying and charitable activities that are undertaken.

In the church as in the world, this is a generation of

words, noise and endless activity that is mostly quite futile. Surely, if such things as those I have enumerated could bring the church of God to maturity and fullness, and vast multitudes to repentance and faith, we would be there before now.

No, no, no! What God declares is that he responds to faith rather than to human effort. Man's best will never do, even if a myriad of us worked ourselves to death almost. Throughout history, again and again God has shown what he can accomplish in a moment, so to speak, that wonderfully pleases and glorifies him. There has to be a higher way—and each of us needs to find it for ourselves. We need heaven's best more than ever before. Never settle for less!

I am not contending for idleness or laziness. Far from it! This is a call to walk in the Spirit, responding wholeheartedly to whatever He directs. "To be walking in what we are hearing" is something I felt to be the challenge for me years ago, and it still is. Too many walk in what has been heard in the past, in what is compatible with acceptable doctrinal norms, or is simply imposed by some church leadership. Many have told us that God speaks to each of us through the Scriptures, through circumstances and through other people. Actually it is only when any one of those ways becomes personalized by being internalized by the Holy Spirit that we have the 'now' word of God for us.

Let the younger generation hear this: "This is a tremendous day for adventure and discovery. Go for it!" I take the counsel of a highly esteemed and deeply loved brother in Christ, Dr. Jack Gray, who is many years my senior. He has wisely and rightly written that "there are many today whom some have described as church-forsakers, but who are actually church-discoverers." We refuse to blindly follow the traditions of men, choosing rather to seek and find for ourselves exactly what God's plan is for us at the present time.

Better Than Revival

HERE IS PART OF A LETTER WE RECEIVED a few days ago, almost fifty years after my visit to Rajnandgaon. Neil had asked what I thought about revival. I shared some of the things written in this chapter.

"We had a significant and moving time with you and Mary yesterday. Thank you for sharing about your time in India—it was a privilege to hear of it, see its impact on you and share in the revelation and impartation of God's Grace. It has quickened a desire to be part of such a revival. It also explains a lot to me. Not having experienced anything greater, I have struggled at times to see the structured church in quite the terms you have seen it. We can read about heaven's visitations, hear about them second or third hand, but it is no substitute for being there—though it was pretty close yesterday. It would certainly spoil someone for anything less."

I have written that tasting heaven's best spoils one from being satisfied with man's best efforts. Seasons of revival are just that—for a season. It is what continues after such a season that is important.

Whether we are ever privileged to be part of a revival situation or not, we can—and indeed, must—taste heaven's best to the extent that we will never settle for man's best. Let me share incidents from my own life that enable one to live a 'better than revival' life style.

Firstly, choosing to place—and keep—the highest priority in my life for an ongoing intimate love relationship with our precious Redeemer. Make no mistake about it, without that all of our activities, beliefs and achievements are nothing more than a "gong booming or a cymbal clashing."

Secondly, coming to a place where I said a big "Yes!" to the Lord Jesus—a "Yes!" that lasts a lifetime. Thereafter the question is never whether something seems to be better, wiser, more reasonable, more acceptable or more effective. It is simply whether it is what God chooses for me at the moment, or not.

Thirdly, as an extension of the big "Yes", being committed to radical obedience to God. Obviously that was behind my daring to speak to that elder in Rajnandgaon.

A God-filled Nobody

Years ago, when I was a Baptist minister I dreamed one Saturday night that Glen Turner, the New Zealand cricket captain told me that I was to bat for New Zealand. In my dream I remonstrated with him about it, but Glen simply said, "Don't worry where the ball goes, don't worry where the Indians [the opposing team] are, just keep your eyes on me, and when I call you be running."

I knew this dream was a message from the Lord. To my shame, in spite of that, when He called me in the Service the next evening, I stood my ground and did not run. A few days later I told my co-pastor Fred that the Holy Spirit had spoken to me in the gathering, telling me to lead the people in singing in the Spirit. "You can't do that!" he said. "The people aren't ready for it."

I told him that I hadn't thought it was a good idea either, but had now committed myself to respond to every prompting of the Spirit from then on, regardless of the consequences. The Lord soon tested me on that commitment and over the years has tested my willingness from time to time, checking that I remain steadfastly willing to do what He asks even when natural reason cannot understand.

I recall reading a translation in which Jesus says, "Whatever you pray for, be believing that you have received, and you will receive." On the basis of that, I chose to believe that I was the recipient of abundant grace, had been brought into a deep and intimate one-ness with the Lord Jesus, and that I would be kept in a continuing state of triumphant freshness. I determined that I should, and would by God's grace alone, be a one-man walking revival, while others may be satisfied to keep on hoping and trusting that they may experience such a thing sometime in the future.

All of this is hugely audacious for a 'nobody', is it not? In spite of my limitations and imperfections Father has been more to me and done more for me than I had ever asked or imagined.

Let us never forget that God our heavenly Father is exceedingly generous. I am confident that you, like me, know experientially that He loves to give good gifts to His children. From time to time we have experienced showers of blessing, fresh stirrings, sweet anointings, wonderful enablings, touches of glory, amazing awareness of His immediate presence, grace for every situation and every need and absolute immersion in His love and peace.

A God-filled Nobody

For a moment if you will, link these special times of outpoured grace with thoughts of revival. Think of a rocket being launched into space. Revival and other divine blessings are like the after-burner of a rocket—not needed permanently, but simply intended to launch us into a higher dimension in our walk and oneness with the Lord Jesus. As with a rocket, there may need to be further brief adjustments to direction and speed, bringing us into the fullness of God's purpose for each of us. Surely Father's desire is for us to enjoy an 'orbital' experience of being seated with Christ in the unseen but very real heavenly realms in Christ Jesus, wonderfully released from the inordinate grip of earthy attraction.

In Essex a brother came to me during a 'tea or coffee break' in a Sunday morning service. He needed help, he told me, because when he had set his eyes on Jesus and gave priority to walking with Him, his pastor had rebuked him for not being faithful enough to the church and all of its activities. When he gave himself to that, his walk with the Lord suffered, and he felt that he was 'drying up' spiritually.

A pastor in America wrote to me at one time saying that he knew I would never tell one of 'his' people to leave 'his' church. But calling believers to give utmost priority to a love relationship with Christ, and to respond to every prompting of the Holy Spirit had led to their leaving. It reminds me of a reference a church leader gave me once. It started, "We regret that the Lord has called John to leave. . ."!

Let me make this very plain. We need one another in the body of Christ. We need the fellowship, inspiration and encouragement that we can bring to one another. We need to meet with other believers whenever and however the Lord, the Head of the church directs. But we most definitely do not need the repetitive, man-initiated activities, the man-controlled 'church' systems, or the imposed sense of obligation to 'the work' and the routine of busy-ness that come with these.

There is a higher way! There is a way to live a New Testament quality of life regardless of our circumstances. With Christ at the very centre of our lives there is abundant grace available for us to live radiant and triumphant lives. Peace like a river and joy unspeakable and full of glory can flood our lives day by day. To enter into the Christian walk I have endeavoured to describe, and to remain there, of course, is better than experiencing a season of revival. In this we are spoiled from being satisfied with man's best, as we enjoy the repeated taste of heaven's best for our lives. Go for it, for Jesus' sake!

More about Rajnandgaon

ONE MAN WHO TURNED TO CHRIST IN faith that day had a reputation of being the most scurrilous and evil man, "the worst sinner" that anyone there knew. A miracle of God's wonderful love and redeeming grace took place. That man began walking down the dusty streets, calling out to attract people's attention and then declaring, "You all know me, you know Victor Das, you know how I have lived, but Jesus has saved me, Jesus has changed me."

He would urge those around him to repent of their selfish, sinful ways and trust in the Lord Jesus. In a part of India where there was opposition to Christianity at that time, and where Christians were imprisoned on trumped up charges, men responded to Victor Das' call and knelt right there in the dusty village street to hand over control of their lives to God. Wonderful!

There were times when I walked down the small business area and was called over by one Hindu businessman or another who wanted to inquire about things I had shared in the tent meeting the previous evening. Had I really said that neither Prime Minister Nehru, nor the Queen of England, nor the New Zealand Prime Minister, nor anyone else in the whole world could reach heaven except through personal faith in the Lord Jesus Christ? I had, and it caught their attention.

News spread into the surrounding areas as people who had discovered the wonder of life in Christ spread the good news. Night after night crowds thronged in to hear the word of God and respond to it.

One evening, part way through my speaking two policemen marched into the tent and up the centre aisle. I told them to sit down, which they promptly did, and I continued speaking to those gathered. When I gave a Gospel invitation for people to come forward, those policemen stood up and ran out of the tent. We were told later that they had been sent to arrest me. At some stage of the crusade the chief of police in the area sent a message to us. Receiving it second or third hand I cannot give an accurate report of it but it seemed to be along these lines: "Tell that man he can have the town. I am going away until he leaves, because I do not want to become a Christian."

At one stage we received a message from a Bible store in Nagpur which was, I think, a couple of hours away by train. We were asked to announce that nobody should go down to buy Bibles until they imported more. They had sold every copy they had. The delightful thing about this was that we had not even mentioned the value of having a Bible, let alone suggested that people buy a copy. Our emphasis had been the God of the word, rather than the word of God.

Late one night a young Sikh man came to talk to David and me. Six days a week he worked until 10 p.m. On his free night he had walked by our well-lit tent to see what was going on. His first question was, "Who is this Jesus you were talking about?" It was a high privilege to share the good news of Christ's coming, and His atoning death on the Cross, to someone who had never heard it before. Time and again Mohindar Singh came back to talk with us.

All Sikhs have the surname Singh, meaning Lion. These turbaned people are a warrior race. I understand that few have ever become Christians.

One evening Mohindar told us that he now wanted to yield his life to the Saviour, which he did. Another evening when he came back to hear more about living for the Lord he mentioned that a fellow Sikh had seen him sitting with us on the open verandah outside our bedroom. He had been warned that if he continued coming to see us and persisted in his purpose of being a Christian he would be put to death rather than being permitted to shame his family.

I immediately said, "Come inside with us so nobody will see you." His unforgettable reply was, "No. Didn't I tell you that I was willing to live for Christ, and willing to die for Him too? Let us stay out here to show that I am not ashamed of being His follower."

After some time Mohindar, whom we had really come to love and appreciate as a brother in the Lord, left Rajnandgaon to visit his parents who lived some distance away. We never saw him again. When we asked about him we were told that his family had 'dealt with him'. Locals made inquiries in his home area with no definite results but with a strong impression that he was no longer alive.

One morning at ten or eleven o'clock the sky darkened rapidly and torrential rain began to fall. I couldn't understand it because the monsoon rains were not due for a couple of months. We rushed out to lower the huge bamboo poles at one corner of our flat-topped tent. It was backbreaking because of the rapidity with which the tent sagged with the weight of water trapped on top.

When I asked about that one day of rain I was told, "Oh those are the mango showers." Apparently without those few hours of rain mangoes would not be able to produce their fruit. How could God and nature organize such a thing? I do not know, but perhaps there is encouragement for someone through the mention of this.

That all of these events flood my memory after so long a time is an indication of how deeply I was affected by them, even though I was only 22 or 23 years of age at the time. Please understand that in it all our focus must not be on a particular expression of God's moving, no matter how wonderful it may be, but rather on God's wonderful love and amazing grace and power. How glorious He is! I can only explain my involvement at such a time in the fact that God loves—and chooses—to use a nobody, "Things that are not," so that He rightly gets all the credit and all the glory. "That no flesh should glory in His presence." To Him alone be the honour and praise and glory for ever and ever. Amen!

A God-filled Nobody

Let me share some brief comments about two other Sikhs who turned to Christ. I had the privilege of meeting Bakh Singh in the twin cities of Hyderabad and Secundrabad. After hearing him speak at a large tent meeting we were invited to stay for lunch. Bakh Singh gave me the privilege of sitting beside him. He was a much loved and honoured man.

We sat cross-legged on the ground to eat our plate of curry and rice with our fingers. No forks were provided. When Indians eat like that their hands only touch the food up to the first joint of their finger, most of the hand staying clean. As soon as I took my first mouthful Bakh Singh quietly told me that I must use my other hand. I am left handed in spite of the way teachers tried to change that when I was a lad at school. He explained that Indians use their left hand for unclean things and their right hand for food.

I quickly licked the fingers my left hand clean and began eating with my right hand. The curry was so hot that tears were running down my face and my nose needed attention. Imagine my struggle to get my handkerchief out of my right trouser pocket with my left hand. I had much to learn.

Sadhu Sundar Singh

I AM CONFIDENT THAT THERE ARE STILL BOOKS available about Sadhu Sundar Singh, even though he lived before my time. Reading about him has been a tremendous inspiration to me in the past, and to ever so many others around the world. Every young person should try to find a copy to read. Here is one story about him:

Sadhu Sundar Singh was hiking with a companion from northern India over a narrow, winding, mountainous track into Tibet. It was freezing cold and snow began falling heavily so that their very lives were at risk. As they trudged on they stumbled over a fellow traveller who had fallen exhausted and was already being covered with snow. When the sadhu asked his companion to help carry him to their destination the companion refused. "If we do that we will also die," he said.

The companion hurried on but Sadhu Sundar Singh lifted the unconscious man onto his back and gradually made his way forward. At a point where walking became easier and the snowfall lessened the sadhu found his companion who had hurried on ahead. He had frozen to death, whereas the extra effort and warmth of carrying the stranger had saved Sadhu Sundar Singh's life, and the stranger's as well.

Well may we recall the words of Jesus, "Whoever will seek to save his life shall lose it but whoever will give his life for my sake and the Gospel's shall save it." There is a cross in Christianity and a cross in the daily life of the believer. Avoid the cross at your peril. Jesus said, "If any man will come after me, let him take up his cross daily and follow me."

Billy Graham in India

WHEN BILLY GRAHAM CAME TO INDIA I was given the opportunity to train counsellors and be responsible for counselling and follow-up work for his crusade in Trivandrum in Travacore, Cochin. That is in India's south-western tip. Quite a privilege!

When leaders gathered at the start of the crusade a bishop told me that my counselling methods had been insulting to his people, especially the clergy, because I had started the sessions with a simple outline of the Gospel. "You act as if my men are un-converted" he said, "We don't need the Gospel."

At that very moment I saw two of the ministers in question walking about fifty paces away. They had both been very grateful because the sessions had not only trained them for counselling, but had also brought them into the reality of life in Christ. "Ask them" I said. The bishop walked away.

Most of the church leaders were very welcoming and graciously supportive. However there was one other bishop who challenged me about our follow-up procedure. Since I have used that term a couple of times let me share with you that to me the first and most important part of follow-up work is the ministry of the Holy Spirit. He seeks to breathe fresh life into the newborn believer, strengthen his love relationship with the Lord Jesus and lead him in fuller understanding of God's ways.

The bishop questioned my procedure. I told him that within 24 hours of a person making a decision for Christ we had posted a letter to their church informing them of the event, forwarded further literature to the person concerned, and sent information to the nearest prayer cell. All across that area there were vibrantly alive prayer groups that my host, a revered and godly K.V. Cherian, was deeply involved with.

The bishop told me that he would make sure that we were blocked from informing those prayer cells. Because I knew they were the best hope of the new spiritual life being nourished, I told him that the moment he did that I would walk away, and he could take over the work I was doing. He knew I was working long hours and left me to it!

Arrangements had been made for my hospitality to be provided at the same hotel the Billy Graham team was in. I asked one of those men how many people he estimated were attending the nightly meetings. He told me that they never included standing people because there was no way to get an accurate measure of their number. People were seated in a very large field and then who knows how many more stood around the edges. As I remember, the estimate was in excess of half a million, a vast sea of humanity.

One morning at that nice hotel I ordered eggs for breakfast. I saw people who came to the dining room after me being served and virtually finishing their meal, but I was served nothing. The waiters seemed to be avoiding me. Eventually I got hold of one and asked him what was going on. His reply was that each time they cooked eggs for me they found they were 'off' and so had to throw them out, clean everything up and start over again. Needless to say I changed my order!

Staying with the team was Dr. Robert Pierce, the founder of World Vision International. I had met him in Bombay and it was a privilege to chat with him again. One day he asked Billy Graham to have his photo taken with me, which he did. Bob had told

Billy, "This is for World Vision." Some time after I eventually returned to New Zealand Dr. Frank Phillips, the executive secretary of World Vision, flew into Auckland and paid my fare up from Christchurch to meet with him. Bob Pierce more clearly manifested the love of Christ than any man I have ever met. Frank Phillips was a kind and gracious man. However I decided not to follow the path for my life that they wanted to make possible.

At one stage during the counsellor training period David Appavoo and I were billeted at a Bible College where I agreed to speak to the students on several occasions. After the first night at that college I asked David how he had slept. We had a common style of bed which had rope latticed across the frame and a mattress under an inch thick. It was just a thick mat really. I was totally surprised by David's answer. No, he hadn't slept well at all. It had been a bad night for him. "I am not accustomed to this kind of comfort" he said. Comfort? Hardly!!!

The bishop who had jurisdiction over that Bible college later requested that I stay on in India and take charge of the college. Not likely! It certainly wasn't for me.

Other Places

AFTER A MONTH IN NORTHERN HYDERABAD State I took a train ride which started before day break, to move on to my next appointment. As soon as the train started out I reached into the inside pocket of my jacket. My wallet was gone. I remembered that the man sitting beside me in that very crowded carriage had jumped up and gone down the corridor, but returned soon after. When I reported my loss to a railway policeman he berated me for providing temptation to poor Indian people. At that time I only had a few dollars [rupees] anyway, and my passport was not in the wallet.

One of the questions I was frequently asked by strangers was, "How much does your government pay you to come here?" They were certain that I was being handsomely paid for it, and could not conceive any other reason for my being in India.

Several hours later I reached my destination and was met by a missionary whom I grew to know and appreciate. He and his wife were gracious hosts. One day he and I set out on bicycles to attend an annual Hindu religious festival or Mela. We cycled for hours, although at times we had to carry our bikes across streams and up banks. There were no roads whatever. At last we reached a place where there was a huge three-storey temple. It was out in a jungle clearing with no habitation in sight, but immense crowds had gathered, some walking for days to reach the place.

Once a year the god in the temple was brought out on a very large cart drawn by numerous men, paraded around a bit and then returned to its temple. The crush of the crowd pressing in towards the god, which itself was a couple of storeys high, was almost frightening. I ended up right against that thing and will never forget the deluge of rice that hit us as people threw it to satisfy their god and gain favour from it. Some of those people were obviously extremely poor so that their offering was most sacrificial.

The missionary and I gave out literature, sought to share the Gospel with all who would listen, and then returned home at the end of a very long and tiring day. We had done all we could. That was one night when I went to bed with a deep cry within me, "Lord, how is it possible for multitudes like that to be given an adequate opportunity to find eternal life?" I was thinking of the Bible verse saying about the Lord Jesus, *"Salvation is found in no one else, for there is no other name under heaven, given to men by which we must be saved."*

Often when I stayed in a place I would go out walking just to be on my own to 'see what I could see' and to think and pray. On every rise or hill or high place someone has placed a shrine or at least piled a few stones together. I confess I tipped them over and scattered them now and again. Don't ask what would have happened if I had been caught! No one who knew me could deny that I was a zealous young man totally committed to serving my Lord. These shrines caused me to think of the heathen high places mentioned in the Old Testament.

All kinds of religions will build something 'sacred' on a high place. Is it a futile effort to get closer to God? Blessed be God that, in contrast to men's vain attempts to climb higher to reach Him, He came to us in the birth, life, crucifixion and resurrection of our precious Lord Jesus. He still comes to us in the Person of the Holy Spirit, abiding in the heart of believers.

A God-filled Nobody

Here in New Zealand churches are frequently built on the highest point and most visible spot in our towns and cities. Look around you, wherever you live. Just as I saw in India, religious buildings in the western world, no less than in the East or in Asia, are built tall, often with spires making them the highest point around. Here, in our home city of Christchurch, the city centre Anglican cathedral has a spire. For the first half of our own life-time city by-laws forbade any other building being erected quite that tall, but that no longer applies. Christianity may have provided many magnificent buildings, but in the process has surely moved far from the simplicity of life in Christ as envisaged in the New Testament, hasn't it?

Mainly in Bombay, but in other places as well, such as Madras [Chennai, now] we gave out lapel pins to young witnessing Christians. They had a question mark on them and nothing else. I found for myself that whether waiting for a bus, standing in a bank queue, riding on a train or just about anywhere else someone would ask, "What is the question?"

It was a lovely opportunity to share the good news of life in Christ. If a question relating to that were asked in New Zealand, everyone else in the queue would most probably pretend not to hear. In India everyone is aware of the spiritual dimension to life and will happily join in a discussion even from up and down a bank queue.

Annual Assemblies

A CANADIAN, AN AUSTRALIAN AND I WERE invited to speak at a church's annual assembly somewhere in central India I think. It was the Basle Mission Church, which had come into being through the efforts of Swiss missionaries. Some considerable time before, [some years, I think] the missionaries had all returned to Switzerland, feeling that their task was complete. They handed everything over to local Christians. It should be obvious that the sooner non-nationals can pass on their work to mature national believers, the healthier it is for all concerned.

I was selected to speak at the gathering on the first evening. My message centred round Christ's provision of salvation for us. When I invited people to surrender their lives to the Lord, irrevocably turning over the rest of their lives to his control and trusting him for salvation, so many responded that I thought perhaps they hadn't understood me. I went over it again and then told them to go home, kneel by their beds and tell the Lord that they were taking that step there and then. I then suggested that they put it in writing and bring the paper back the next morning. Ninety-nine pieces of paper were brought back.

We three speakers shared a large room in a building that had once been a missionary's home. Before I went to that first meeting I undid my bedroll, took out my mosquito net, hung it on the four corner poles attached to my bed, and tucked it in. We only had candles to light the room when we returned there.

When I came back from the meeting the other two men were already there, but my mosquito net had been removed. I asked the Canadian, "John, did you take my net?" He replied that it wasn't mine, but his. He believed that I had taken it from his home when I had previously stayed there. As I told him, I had had it and my bed-roll since before he had come to India.

I tried to sleep totally covered by my sheet. It was too hot to have other bedding. By morning my face was swollen with multiple mosquito bites. I suspect that is where I contracted the malaria that plagued me off and on for many years afterwards. John never told me whether he found his own net or not. I know that he had not intentionally harmed me.

Soon after my arrival in India I read a small book entitled, "God came to Gujerat." That is a region in western India. It was a story about revival. Reading of such happenings has always thrilled me. I have often been stirred by a longing deep within me for the church of God to know experientially an on-going joyously vibrant life, being continually controlled by the Holy Spirit. Not only that, but also for every member to be walking in an intimate love relationship with our dear Lord Jesus, and for precious lost people to be being brought to the Saviour.

It was a thrill to be invited to speak at the annual Assembly of the Mission group in the area of Gujerat mentioned in that book. I wanted to sit at the feet of brothers and sisters who had enjoyed such overwhelming blessing. I expected the revival to be continuing, but alas there was no sign of it. People were willing to share about events two or three years previously, but had nothing fresh and up-to-date to talk about. It seemed to David and me that they had just about reverted to the way of 'playing churches' that they had engaged in previously.

For five or six days I spoke in the gatherings of

delegates from local churches, but it seemed as if there was no response whatever in the hearts of the listeners. David and I searched our own hearts, wept and prayed.

On the Sunday afternoon as I was speaking I became aware of a new 'quickening' among the people. To be honest, I hate afternoon meetings. People tend to be sleepy, and especially on Sundays, probably heavy with their noon dinner.

I cannot tell you how it happened, or even exactly what was said, but it seemed as though a breath of fresh air swept through that church building. People began getting down on their knees. In seconds my interpreter was on his face before the Lord. Thinking that I should continue speaking and yet not knowing what to do, I turned around to ask the Mission leader. To my surprise, everyone on the platform, including the leader, was also on their knees or on their faces. I shook him, but he didn't seem to know I was there.

Then the penny dropped! Our sovereign God was at work and had made sure that I couldn't interfere by removing my interpreter. What did I do? I was glad that there was an open window at one end of the platform. I jumped out of it and went for a long walk, communing with the Lord and blessing Him for His amazing grace.

Yes, there was repentance. Everyone realized where they had missed the mark, and re-committed themselves to keep on walking in what the Holy Spirit was revealing to them. Our train left town that same night at about 1am, I think. The platform was crowded with exuberant believers singing joyfully to and about their wonderful Lord. Glory!

A Unique Opportunity

AT ONE TIME I WAS ON A LONG TRAIN JOURNEY down to Madras, though I cannot recall where the journey began. I believe I boarded in the afternoon and arrived sometime around the middle of the next day. For the entire journey only one other person shared my compartment. He was a high caste Brahmin who proudly showed me autographed photos of Pundit Jawalharlal Nehru, the India Prime Minister, and other high officials. I think one of them was his uncle, but I am not totally sure which one.

My fellow passenger asked me what I was in India for, and I tried to answer with a clear and yet non-confrontational reply. When he began telling me the differences between Hinduism and Christianity, I interposed something else. Since we were to spend many hours together I suggested that we try and discover any similarities there may be, starting with the nature of God. "Yes," he agreed, the world about us and the universe at large prove that God is mighty and powerful. "What about orderliness?" I asked, before moving on to the beauty and wisdom revealed in nature.

A God-filled Nobody

Our conversation went on and on, stopping for a while—perhaps at a station—and then continued again. Eventually I asked if we could see that a Supreme Being like that would want to communicate with the creatures he had made, and to reveal himself to us. Well, Hinduism has had various supposed incarnations. I had previously seen several temples, shrines and pools dedicated to their God Krishna. Although most people never saw him, priests [sadhus] reported a number of times in history that Krishna had appeared and 'dallied with the maidens'. It was intended to explain various inexplicable pregnancies!

Our final area of discussion was the provision of freedom from sin's guilt and power. He talked of pilgrimages to the Ganges and so on. Do you know that some precious and yet benighted people go many miles 'measuring their length' in an effort to find appeasement and release from sin and guilt? To measure their length they lay prostrate on the ground, marked where their head had reached, stood up, put their feet there and again prostrated themselves and marked where there head reached, and so forth, on and on.

The opportunity came to share the gospel with

this well educated and highly intelligent person. Then came our dilemma. "How can we prove who is right?" he asked me. My reply surprised myself. It was "That is quite simple. As I share about salvation in Christ with you a voice within you is telling you that this is right, it is the truth." He told me in all honesty that he could not deny the inner voice, but added as a delayed afterthought that it was probably just the influence of my personality.

My final question to that fine gentleman was whether he thought that the influence would continue for 24 or 48 hours after he left the train. He knew that if it was simply my influence it would quickly fade. I just as surely knew that since it was the Holy Spirit, [acting in what theologians have called 'prevenient grace'—the grace that goes before] that He would tug at his heart and refresh his memory long after we had parted.

Over the years since then I have challenged all kinds of unbelievers with that same thought and the reality of it has never been denied. No matter if they were Hindus, Muslims, atheists or know-it-all super educated 'egg-head' types they could not deny that inner voice.

This principle applies to the Holy Spirit speaking within Christians too. Sadly many try to drown out that voice by repeating the 'mantra' of their doctrinal position or some such thing. It has been wonderful to speak to individuals and gatherings of people in many parts of the world, all the while maintaining a sure confidence in the Holy Spirit's efforts to draw people into fullness in Christ.

One time when we went down to South Africa from Ireland—both of which I will write more later—someone asked me what was the strongest impression I came away with from Ireland. The answer was simple, "I am more than ever convinced and deeply impressed with how much God loves sinful Irishmen." Surely it is not difficult to count on God at work within everyone we know and everyone we meet, seeking to show His glorious, immeasurable love by seeking to draw them to Himself. You can stake your life on that!

Some Other Memories

WHILE I WAS IN RAJNANDGAON THE leader of a Mennonite mission, Bishop Weaver, came to at least one of the meetings. As a result of that I was invited to come and speak in their Mission church, which came about some time later. These lovely people welcomed us warmly and David and I thoroughly enjoyed our time among them. I cannot remember much about the actual meetings, but I do recall the whole appreciative crowd who bade us farewell with joyous and wholehearted gratitude.

I was staying with the doctor of their quality hospital. One day he invited me into the operating theatre to watch him operate on a couple of people. I suppose he had obtained permission first. A most interesting experience!

One day Bishop Weaver and his wife took me in their land rover to visit some fairly remote Indian Christians. There were no formed roads for part of the journey, but the Bishop knew where he was going. At one point he was driving over a grass area that was a little slick with moisture—dew or rain, I do not remember. He spun his steering wheel and did what today's youth call donuts. I couldn't believe it! The Bishop's wife expressed her displeasure.

Coming over a rise, or around a corner, we suddenly came upon a herd of goats being led along by a young Indian fellow. Before he could stop the bishop hit and killed one of the goats. The herdsman was very angry and demanded full compensation. For a minute or two the bishop 'played' with him saying that he had only harmed the head, so would only pay for that. However he paid full price and left the herdsman with his dead goat. Just as well it wasn't on a busy thoroughfare or in a major market. In places like that to maim or kill a sacred animal could cause a riot and put your lives in danger.

Many years later Mary and I visited a place in Pennsylvania where the Mennonites have built a fascinating replica of the Tabernacle Moses was instructed by God to make. When I mentioned to a Mennonite lady there that I had met Bishop Weaver in India she enthusiastically spoke of him as one of their outstanding leaders. His keen sense of humour would have been an asset, I am sure.

Although I have no idea of the setting, I have clear memory of going out with an Australian missionary in his jeep as he visited some remote villages. It was extremely hot that day, but the Ozzie looked great in his freshly ironed white safari suit. At one village he asked about a certain man, then quickly turned to me and said, "Come." He had been told that the man was dead.

We went to a little circular mud walled, thatched roof, one-roomed hut. As we approached the open door the stench was shocking. My friend did not hesitate one second. He stooped down and entered the low entrance. There was an old man there in an appalling condition. He picked him up in his arms, washed and cleaned him up, gently pouring water through his open lips.

What a mess! In that place when a person in a Hindu family was thought to be dying the rest of the family moved out of the 'house' into another, and left him alone to die. After that nobody entered the place. They just came to the doorway and threw a bit of food in to him.

South India Again

THE LARGEST GATHERINGS I SPOKE AT were in South India, perhaps up to 20,000 or so. But they were by no means the largest gatherings I attended, even apart from the Billy Graham Crusade. There are a few months in some parts of Travancore—Cochin when seasonal work has been completed and there is little or no work to do. Christians dubbed this the Convention Season.

Joe Weatherly had warned me ahead of time what it was like to preach at a Mar Thoma church convention. This is a church that believes it was founded by the apostle Thomas. They have buildings dating earlier than the tenth or eleventh centuries, I believe. At the first meeting Joe had addressed he had spoken for forty-five minutes. The presiding bishop asked him to speak longer, but he had nothing else to say. So the bishop rounded it off with another hour and a half or so.

At these gatherings people wander in and out at will, and some don't arrive for ages after it begins. Mind you, they may have walked for hours to get there. The first time I spoke, everyone spontaneously broke out into singing when I was in the midst of some point or other. I'd been speaking for about thirty minutes, but assumed that they'd had enough. Not so. They just burst out into song whenever they feel like it and then settle down for further preaching.

Mar Thoma Sunday morning services last ever so long because of all the ceremonies and rituals they go through. At one stage this includes the waving of incense all around the place. They also practice a kiss of peace, which is nothing like you might imagine. I'll try to explain it. The officiating priest turns from the altar, presses his two hands together and holds them out. His assistant 'wipes' his hands down the priest's hands, turns and holds out his hands to someone else. The same procedure flows right down the congregation until everyone has both received and imparted this so called kiss of peace.

There had been a time when the Mar Thoma church had been cold, formal, and lifeless. In probably the only record ever of a denomination turning back to a higher, purer path, there came a time when they once more believed and proclaimed the Gospel of salvation and encouraged believers to live godly lives.

A God-filled Nobody

At the Marama Convention crowds reached 120,000 or more. Poles were erected in a dry river-bed and palm fronds were inter-twined over these to provide shade. Let me add that in some southern areas I met youngsters up to 15 or 16 years of age who had never seen rain. That is drought!

In earlier days they had a novel method of having a speaker heard by these large crowds. Some way down among the crowd someone would be appointed to stand and repeat what the speaker had said. Further down someone else would relay what that person had said, and so on. It must have been interesting!

Of course by the time I was there a public address system was used. However a remnant of the old system remained. Standing right beside the speaker was someone who repeated exactly what the speaker had just said, using the same tone of voice, gestures and so on. People loved it, describing it as a second blessing. Many Christians would declare that there is a far more important second blessing than that.

At the Marama Convention I had opportunity for enjoyable chats with, among others, Dr. E. Stanley

Jones. There was a time in my life when I found his books both interesting and worthwhile reading. He certainly was an excellent speaker. He had been a friend of Mahatma Gandhi. Previously several missionaries had warned me that in their eyes Dr. Jones was a heretic who had even said that the Mahatma had gone to heaven even though he died a Hindu. I asked him about it. He replied that what he had said, while Gandhi was alive, was that heaven would be poorer if he didn't go there. He would say that about anyone alive he said. I don't know if I can theologically accept the idea of 'heaven being a poorer place' for any reason whatever, but who could challenge Dr. Jones desire for everyone to be saved?

You will laugh at this! At one stage as I stayed with some Indian folk in an area where some people had never seen a European, I was dubbed "The white, white man." Around there, as in many other parts of village India, when people wanted to wash—and they do keep themselves clean—they would go to a village well and draw up a bucket of water. Somehow they could chastely wash every part without taking off their clothes.

To be helpful to me my hosts rigged up some

matting on their property so that I had that around me. They provided me with a bucket of warm water. Great! I went in, closed the matting squares, removed my clothes and had a good wash. At one stage I thought I heard a noise behind me and turned around quickly. There were several pairs of eyes peeping through the corner of the mats. It quickly closed, and just as quickly I turned around to see eyes ogling me from a different corner. Embarrassing! I didn't take long to wash after that!

When I asked my hosts about it they said that people simply could not believe that a person could be white all over. They just had to check it out!

When Mary and I first started going out together I mentioned in all sincerity that it wouldn't be wise for any girl to marry me. I was committed to following the Lord wherever he took me and I knew that could possibly mean only having temporary places of abode, be involved with missionary work or something of the kind. She replied, "We could take as the text of our life Matthew 6:33." In the translation we used in those days, this read, *"Seek ye first the kingdom of God and his righteousness, and all these things will be added unto you."*

In the midst of our courtship I went to India for two years. This meant that we wrote many letters to each other. I stayed with an Indian family at one place in South India. I came home one day and was told that a letter had arrived for me. It was from Mary, and had already been opened. When I asked about it the man replied, "Of course. I am the head of the house and so I open and read all mail that comes into it." In a metaphorical sense I immediately beheaded him on that particular point! Who knows what the 'sweet nothings' of a western love letter might seem like to a village Indian?

I must share another unforgettable memory with you. I spent a week at the place where Amy Carmichael had worked for many years saving girls from infancy to young womanhood from temple prostitution. These innocent victims of a false religion are handed over by parents for this immoral purpose. There were between 1,500 an 1,800 girls there when I visited.

Dohnavur was a lovely place that I reached by bus, coming over miles of parched and arid land. This was like an oasis. There were lovely shade trees, green fields, productive gardens, and their own orchard. Missionaries of various denominations and from quite a number of countries served there, providing love homes for these dear children.

They were an entire village with their own residential area, church, school, workshops, and I don't remember what else. While I was there the funeral was held for an old lady who had been the last child Amy Carmichael had rescued in her lifetime. The service was held in the morning with the body lying on a flat board and totally covered with blossoms. In the evening everyone gathered in the church simply to sing songs about heaven. It was truly precious. As usual, when I recognised a tune I joined in, even though I did not know the language they were singing in.

The first lunch time I was in Dohnavur I gathered with others in a dining hall. The meal began and every one was chatting happily. Suddenly there was silence—almost. Everyone stopped talking, except me, though I did stop quite quickly!

I learned what it was about. In the centre of the village there was the worship centre which had a clock in the spire that struck the time every hour. I hadn't even heard the clock striking, but everyone else's ears were tuned in to it. You see, they had a practice that every time the clock struck everyone would pause a moment to thank the Lord for His presence with them and to whisper their love for Him. It seemed to me that the awareness of Christ's presence stayed with them over the full hour, and therefore over the entire day.

I had never known anything like it even though I had read about an individual here or there 'practising the presence of Christ.' It may not be possible to be constantly aware of the Lord's close nearness every moment of the day, since we are all involved with good and necessary things that demand our attention. But we can all probably be much more aware of His presence than we are. Perhaps we can focus our attention God-ward for a moment every time we hear a door shut, or a phone rings, or some such thing. This can please and honour the Lord, and also make a tremendous difference to our daily lives.

Amy Carmichael's Vision

LET ME NOW SHARE TWO OF THE INGREDIENTS into Father's preparation of my heart prior to going to India. The first is a short poem that I learned as a teenager, repeated to myself, and sometimes to others, many times. I have no difficulty in calling it to mind after all the intervening years

Here it is:

O for a passionate passion for souls,
O for a pity that yearns,
O for a love that loves unto death,
O for a fire that burns.

O for a pure prayer power that prevails
That pours itself out for the lost,
Victorious prayer in the Conqueror's name,
O for a Pentecost.

The other factor in the Holy Spirit's preparation of my heart is a vision that Amy Carmichael shared. This is it:

"The tom-toms thumped straight on all night, and the darkness shuddered round me like a living,

feeling thing. I could not sleep, so I lay awake and looked; and I saw, as it seemed, this:

"That I stood on a grassy patch, and at my feet a ravine broke straight down into infinite space. I looked, but saw no bottom; only cloud shapes, black and furiously coiled, and great shadow-shrouded hollows, and unfathomable depths. Back I drew, dizzy at the depth.

"Then I saw forms of people moving toward the edge. There was a woman with a baby in her arms and another little child holding on to her dress. She was on the very edge. She lifted her foot for the next step... Then to my horror, I saw that she was blind. Before I could say anything she was over, and the children with her. Their cries pierced the air as they fell into the inky blackness of the ravine!

"Then I saw more streams of people flowing from all quarters. All were blind, stone blind; all walked straight toward the edge. There were shrieks as they suddenly knew themselves falling, and a tossing up of helpless arms, catching, clutching at empty air. But some went very quietly, and fell without a sound.

"Then I wondered, with a wonder that was sheer

83

agony, why no one stopped them at the edge. I could not. I was glued to the ground, and I couldn't even yell; though I strained and tried, only a whisper would come out.

"Then I saw that along the edge there were sentries set at intervals.

"But the intervals were too large; there were wide, unguarded gaps between. And over these gaps the people fell in their blindness, unwarned; and the green grass seemed blood-red to me, and the ravine yawned like the mouth of hell.

"Then I saw, like a little picture of peace, a group of people under some trees with their backs turned to the ravine. They were making daisy chains. Sometimes when a piercing shriek cut the quiet air and reached them, it disturbed them and they thought it was a rather crude noise. And if one of their group started up and wanted to go and do something to help, then all the others would pull that one down. "Why should you get so excited about it? You must wait for a definite call to go! You haven't finished your daisy chain yet. It would be really selfish," they said, "to leave us to finish the work alone."

"There was another group. It was made up of people whose great desire was to get more sentries out; but they found that very few wanted to go, and sometimes there were no sentries for miles along the edge.

"Once a girl stood alone in her place, waving the people back; but her mother and other relations called, and reminded her that her furlough was due; she must not break the rules. And being tired and needing a change, she had to go and rest for awhile; but no one was sent to guard her gap, and over and over the people fell, like a waterfall of souls. Once a child grabbed at a tuft of grass that grew on the very edge of the ravine; it clung convulsively, and it called—but nobody seemed to hear. Then the roots of the grass gave way, and with a cry the child went over, its two little hands still holding tight to the torn-off bunch of grass. And the girl who longed to be back in her gap thought she heard the little one cry, and she sprang up and wanted to go; at which her friends reproved her, reminding her that no one is necessary anywhere; "The gap would be well taken care of!" they said. And then they sang a hymn.

"Then through the hymn came another sound like

the pain of a million broken hearts wrung out in one full sob. And a horror of great darkness came upon me, for I knew that it was "The cry of blood".

"Then a voice thundered. It was the voice of the Lord, and He said, "What hast thou done? The voice of thy brother's blood crieth unto me from the ground."

"The tom-toms still beat heavily, the darkness still shuddered and shivered about me; I heard the yells of the devil-dancers and weird, wild shrieks of the devil-possessed just outside the gate.

"What does it matter? It has gone on for years; it will go on for years. Why make such a fuss about it? God forgive us!

"God arouse us! Shame us out of our callousness! Shame us out of our sin!" So shared Amy Carmichael.

Yes, my reader, in India I also heard the tom-toms. I felt the darkness, I saw the hopelessness and demon-possessed frenzy of ash-covered dancers, sometimes crying and shouting throughout a long tropical night—collapsing in utter exhaustion or hypnotic trance, only to rise a little later to continue in their benighted madness. At times when I needed rest my head has throbbed with the seemingly endless din of the continuing and repetitive noise of tom-toms and the so-called music of heathen worshippers.

I have seen sin-blinded people worship the creation of men's hands, set out on their futile religious pilgrimages, give their scarce and meagre food supply to a man-made god in hope of some kind of spiritual progress, and act in ugly immoral and depraved ways.

Many a time I have been sickened by empty religious performances and by the self righteousness of daisy chain makers who have been so quick to point out the error, and even the heresy, of anyone who cries, "Enough, there has to be a better and higher way!"

I have seen Christians paddling in the shallows of spiritual mediocrity attempting to denigrate and bring down anyone whose heart is set on "waters deep enough to swim in." Back then as now, I recalled the Apostle Paul saying, "I stand at Caesar's judgement seat" and I have declared within myself, "I stand at Jesus judgement seat." My keenest efforts have been so paltry, but I have wept and prayed and cared very deeply. God have mercy on us all.

The Voyage Home

AFTER MY TWO EVENTFUL YEARS IN INDIA were completed I travelled home on the P & O passenger liner *Himalaya*. One could only marvel at the amazing grace and goodness of God over that time.

That He could use even someone like me was beyond my comprehension then, and is so even more today. Never more than now have I been so conscious of my limitations, imperfections, inadequacies, weaknesses and flaws. In spite of all this God has been extremely merciful and gracious to me, and ever so many believers have shown me kindness and love. This does not mean that I focus undue thought and attention on myself. Far from it! Day by day we continue to enjoy the wonders of Father's love and care and to magnify the Lord in our hearts. He is all and in all.

On board ship I struck up an acquaintance with a fine young Muslim. Now and again we sat on deck chairs and chatted about our backgrounds and interests. He shared with me his understanding of Islam and I spoke to him of Christ. I will never forget his final statement to me. "You have a better religion than I have, for Islam has no Saviour. But I will live and die a Muslim." My prayer was that since God hadn't finished with him yet, he would still come to trust in the Lord Jesus for his personal salvation.

The ship stopped briefly at Colombo, Ceylon, and then headed for Freemantle. From there we headed beneath Australia and across the Great Australian Bight to Sydney. The weather was stormy in the Bight to the extent that a number of people were hurt, one hitting his head as he was pitched into the piano, and another, I think, falling in a gangway or down some steps.

For a day or two, when I went to the dining room hardly anyone else had made it! Although there were barge boards fitted around the table-tops to stop dishes sliding off, I had to grasp the dishes in front of me as quickly as I could whenever the ship rolled or plunged over another wave. I saw dishes flying off one or two other tables where folk were sitting, and food sliding across the floor. In fact I was told that a tremendous number of dishes were smashed over those few days.

It was interesting to sit in a lounge, look to the left

and see a wall of water out the portholes. As the ship lurched a similar wall of water appeared out the portholes on the other side. Quite exciting! I loved it then, but I wouldn't now. I understand that that was the last journey of the Himalaya before stabilisers were fitted.

At Sydney I left the 'Himalaya', and took another passenger ship, the 'Wanganella', across the Tasman sea to Wellington, New Zealand. Mary was waiting for me there, with our good friend Roland Browning. Before the year was out I turned 24, and we were married. So another chapter of life began for us.

A God-filled Nobody

Part 3

New
Zealand

A God-filled Nobody

After India

IN DECEMBER 1956, A FEW MONTHS AFTER I returned from India, Mary and I were married. Our first son Graham was born in Christchurch on 15 October the next year, and our second son, Roger was born in Auckland on 4 August 1960.

In 1957 I took over from Malcolm Miles as director of Youth for Christ in Christchurch, and continued in the position for a couple of years. From there I proceeded with theological studies, and that was followed eventually with some years in a pastoral ministry.

It was always a privilege to introduce someone to the Saviour, and a delight to lead believers into a deeper walk with Christ, but I could never really accept the man-made systems and procedures that seem to be an inevitable part of organized church life. I remember commenting at one stage that for generations churches could get along fairly well without the Holy Spirit being allowed to be God in their midst, but if their committees were taken away they would collapse in confusion.

In my first pastorate I took my pre-school age son

Graham by the hand to walk to the Sunday School which was next door to our home. "Daddy," he said, "I love Jesus, but I hate church," I told him that was perfectly all right, since I sometimes felt like that myself. I wonder how many other children—and adults too, for that matter—feel exactly the same way!

Mary and I have vivid memories of the sinking of the *Wahine* inter-island ferry on 10 April 1968. Mary had gone down to Christchurch from Wellington where we were living at the time, because her mother was close to death. When her mother died and the funeral was arranged I booked a flight to be there, with a kind neighbour agreeing to care for our two young sons.

Before making my booking I phoned Mary to say that I would book a flight back the same evening for both of us. Mary rightly told me that we couldn't really afford it. However, I felt strongly that it was the right thing to do and so it was agreed. I think it was as much out of concern for our boys as anything. That was the last flight to Wellington that evening. If we had taken the boat instead, which would have been the logical thing to do, we would have been on the *Wahine* when it sank. My facetious comment afterwards was that I just couldn't have made it swimming to the shore with Mary on my back!

When the Association of Baptist churches in Canterbury and Westland were celebrating a century of their united witness, I presented a motion to a special meeting. It was that all the committees that had been formed over the last one hundred years be disbanded forthwith, and that the churches return to the simplicity and purity of the original purposes for which the Association was formed.

Don't ask me how, but the motion was duly seconded and carried. Some talked of being on committees for many years, having met together monthly, kept minutes faithfully, made reports regularly, and yet were unable to recall one thing that had been accomplished through their existence. There was a deacon in the Riccarton church where I ministered at the time, who walked around for months shaking his head, looking at me and saying, "Pastor, you don't know what you've done. You don't know what you've done." It didn't take long for committees to begin appearing again.

When I was interviewed prior to being invited to be

the minister at Riccarton, one of the men asked me, "Do you believe in long hair?" He was talking of a fad young men were going through. My concern was to bring people into the kind of vital relationship with the Lord Jesus that they could hear Him for themselves if He was not pleased with anything at all in their lives. I later discovered that the man was head of a Christian school in the area. When he huffed, "It is easy to see you are not a school teacher" I replied that I was not God's policeman either. Besides which I was happy with my boys having hair like that as long as it was clean and tidy.

After I had been at Riccarton for six months or so, several church members began asking me, "When are we going to have our first evangelistic crusade?" My reply was that it would not be until Father showed us His specific plan for this place at this time. I encouraged them to be praying about it.

One night while I was waiting on the Lord I received revelation about it. It began with leaflets that would be put in letterboxes once a week for five weeks. The leaflets had plenty of photos. The first one was headed "A church is people." The fifth leaflet gave notice that during the following week one of us would be calling on them. Our purpose was [1] To share something beautiful and meaningful that the Lord Jesus was doing in our life at that time; [2] To see if there was any way that we could help them; [3] To offer them literature if they would like some.

You will note that we were not inviting anyone to a church service, and nor were we asking anyone to accept the Lord Jesus Christ as their own personal Saviour. Not only were people who were ill or elderly helped in practical ways, but others asked us to share more about salvation with them. In a number of cases people turned to the Lord at that time. Still others came to services and responded to the Gospel call then. Each day we received phone calls from non-church-going people in our district. Other churches in the area also benefited through this effort.

I recall talking to one man at his home. Yes, he wanted to have Christ in his life, but he was an Anglican. I knew that his vicar was a godly evangelical man and so I asked if I could get him to call. He was amazed, but agreed. As soon as I returned home I phoned Chris Parry-Jennings about it. Later that day he called me back to share about his successful visit.

A God-filled Nobody

We began to get calls from other Baptist ministers around the country, asking me to share 'our system, and to send copies of our literature.' My reply was that the system was simple. "Just wait on the Lord until some day or night when you are praying and fasting, the Holy Spirit will give you the unique pattern that there is for your situation." They wanted the details and the literature, which I declined to forward to them. Several said, "Beaumont you're crazy. I'll phone the church secretary and get the stuff."

Alas, all around the world people try to slavishly copy the external aspects of something precious God is doing somewhere else, but too often they miss the heart of it!

While I was pastoring in Hamilton I began to see how much people relied on their ministers, believing that we could hear God in a way that they cannot. I started to tell people that nobody can hear God for you as clearly as you can hear God for yourself.

One Sunday night a fine young man asked if he could make arrangements to see me, his situation was urgent, and he needed counselling. Well, I have tried to be an available man, but I told the fellow that I could see him on Thursday week. "But Pastor

John" he remonstrated, "This is urgent." I told him why I had said Thursday week. "It gives you time to seek God for yourself," I explained. "I will also seek Him for you, and when we come together we will see if we are hearing the same thing." Although a little confused by this he agreed.

The next Sunday he shared with a big grin that he didn't really need to see me Thursday because Father had made things crystal clear for him. Unless we break the kind of spiritual dependence on church leaders and others—such as illustrated in this example—believers will never come to maturity in Christ. Maybe it is 'safer' for leaders if they don't, sadly.

One Sunday night after the service a young woman asked for help in two ways. She was scheduled for spinal surgery within a day or two, and she also wanted to be filled with the Holy Spirit. As we spoke together she was sitting in such a contorted way that I quickly offered a cushion to her. We gave her second request priority, but also asked the Lord to heal her.

I had forgotten the incident, but the next Sunday morning I saw her entering the church building, and noted that she was unusually radiant. In the service I invited her to share a word of testimony. When she had gone to hospital tests showed that she no longer needed surgery, to the doctors' amazement. She gave the credit to the Lord. At the university where she lectured, many unbelievers were even more amazed when she shared what God had graciously done for her. They had known the reality of her condition.

When the service concluded that morning a man who for years had had far too much influence in the place, came to me angrily, exclaiming, "Pastor, we can't have that in a Baptist church!" I replied, "My brother, I am as surprised as you, but it looks as though God can even do that kind of thing in a Baptist church." He loved me not.

Late one Sunday night, in fact after midnight, I was driving home to Hamilton from the Bay of Plenty where I had been speaking in special services, with my wife and our son Roger in the car. Roger was about 15 years of age at the time. As we came down the Waikato side of the Kaimais the road was damp and there was quite a heavy fog so I was driving slowly. Through the fog we saw the blurred light of a vehicle down below us as it made its way to the top.

Not long after that when I drove around a fairly sharp blind bend I saw clearly that there was a station wagon right in front of me, stopped sideways across the road. It blocked the road totally, and I had no chance of stopping. After some minutes I asked Mary and Roger if they had seen what I saw. They both had. I had not had time to brake, and had had no way to dodge the other vehicle. How we passed it is an inexplicable mystery, and yet we had. We were ever so grateful when we eventually arrived home safe and sound.

But there is more yet! Two weeks later we had a visit from a New Plymouth high school teacher that we knew. Almost immediately he asked me, "John what were you doing Sunday night after midnight a couple of weeks ago," stating the date. When I asked the reason for his question he replied that a New Plymouth Christian lady had asked him to enquire. Apparently she had woken up—wide awake—at that time and had felt such a strong urge to get up and pray for us that she promptly responded to the urging, even though she scarcely knew us. No such thing had happened to her before, so she wondered what it was all about. Amazing grace!

It was while we were in Hamilton that a new door

began opening for us. With a grown family we were able to respond to requests for my ministry that started flooding in. Thus I came to an end of one period of my life and moved out into fresh and precious ways to respond to the Holy Spirit's direction for my life. We shared the 'now' word of the Lord in numerous places around New Zealand, including in the township of Fairlie, south of Christchurch, which later became a home base for us as we responded to requests for ministry that came from overseas.

Speaking in general terms, the heart thrust of my ministry over the years has been that every believer might give utmost priority to a continuing love relationship with the Lord Jesus. Following on from that, and essentially linked to it, that they should develop a capacity to clearly hear the inner 'voice' of the Holy Spirit and then to walk in the Spirit day by day, responding to Him in every aspect of their lives. The overflow of such a life-style must surely be an out-flowing of the water of life to the precious thirsty lost ones that are all around us.

Fairlie

I N 1976, WHILE WE WERE LIVING IN HAMILTON, the FGBMFI in New Zealand set up simultaneous evangelistic crusades around the country, with two speakers allocated to each crusade. Their idea was to link a minister from one of the 'main line' churches with a Pentecostal pastor. As a Baptist minister, I agreed to participate in a week of special meetings at the New Life Centre in Timaru.

I was received with wholehearted acceptance, and marvelled at both the warmth and responsiveness of these dear people. We were invited to return again and again, even on one occasion leading the church while the pastor was on a much-needed vacation. Our love link with these folk resulted in our being invited to speak at special meetings in seven or eight other New Life Centres, including the one at Fairlie.

On our first visit to Fairlie I had a strong inner feeling that Father purposed that fellowship to be a place of refuge, a haven for refreshing and to be significant in His purposes even though it appeared to be small, remote and insignificant. I mentioned something about this in a meeting, after which one of the elders asked me if Milton Smith or Jack Lloyd had spoken to me in those terms. They hadn't. Unbeknown to me those men had apparently spoken the same word.

Years later, another elder, Allan Bell, told us about what had blessed him in our very first meeting there. In the first part of the service he could look across diagonally and see me. He couldn't see my face, but kept noticing my hands when they were by my side. A small thing made a deep impression on him. As he saw my hands he realized that I was totally relaxed even though in a very different kind of church 'culture' than I was accustomed to, and had no idea what might happen next.

Mac, the Fairlie New Life pastor invited us back on a number of occasions. Before one of our visits, Allan had been working on his farm when a strong conviction from the Lord caused him to visit the other two elders who were also farmers. "John Beaumont is to be based in Fairlie," he told them, "Moving out from here with an apostolic ministry."

That terminology would probably have been about

as strange to them at that time as it was to me. When they told me about this I simply said that we should leave it with the Lord until He made us aware of the time for its fulfilment. Mac told me that the elders felt that I should become the pastor there, but he knew that I had a wider ministry than that. He obviously didn't understand the message Allan had heard.

The time came when Mac moved to their Centre in Ashburton and, according to New Life custom, he appointed his successor for Fairlie. Many months after that Bevan, the new pastor, phoned me. He had heard that I was going to be in that part of the country, and invited me to spend a week with them. I readily agreed because for weeks I had been carrying a deep heart burden for those people. Often during the day, and at times during the night, I had been earnestly interceding for them, although I had no insight into the reason for it.

A day or two before that visit to Fairlie, Rob, another New Life pastor, told me that Bevan had put the three elders out of eldership, and that there was distress among the people. Within an hour or two of our arrival, Bevan chatted with me about the now ex-elders. Then, and repeatedly over several days, whenever he started to talk with me about those three men, I asked him if he could state that he knew with certainty that by being in Fairlie he was in the centre of Father's will and purpose for him.

How well I remember the reply he finally gave me to my question. It was an unequivocal "No." I interrupted him at that point, quietly saying "I am so glad that you admit that Bevan, because I came here with a word from the Lord for you. You are to leave Fairlie by the end of the month."

"You have no authority to tell me what to do," he told me, somewhat angrily. I assured him that I was well aware that I had no church authority, but that he would not be able to deny that I spoke with heaven's authority. I asked if he knew what he should be doing, and, when he told me, I offered to set the wheels in motion to bring that about. He declined my offer.

At the end of our week there, I drove to Timaru and talked with Rob about the situation. The Fairlie elders were well-respected men. Not only had Bevan denied them their role, but Father's sheep in that place were being distressed and scattered. Rob recognised that I had spoken a true word to Bevan, and backed it up when Bevan contacted him.

At Rob and Mac's request we returned to Fairlie on the last day of the month, at the same time as Bevan and his family left. It was a privilege to give ourselves to the healing of hurts and the restoration of precious people.

After several weeks there at that time, we left Fairlie straight after a Sunday morning service. Prior to the meeting a group of folk were chatting outside the building, especially commenting on the gorgeous day. Someone raised the idea of going down to the river later that afternoon and everyone else liked to idea.

One of the men, realising that their suggested plans meant that they would not be back for the usual evening service, asked me if I thought they should have a meeting by the river. I replied that they wouldn't want to space themselves out at about every fifty yards, so of course they would be meeting. The point was taken, and everyone recognised that friendly informality with their families was 'Service' enough. Where did anyone get the idea that we have a biblical or spiritual obligation to have two church services every Sunday?

The time came when I asked the Fairlie elders to

move the thought of our being based there off the back burner. We all agreed that it was time, and so the move took place. We have many precious memories of our years there—even though it was mostly a home base to return to from our prolonged journeys overseas. I always valued being able to come back home and tell the elders about our ministry journey.

Our memories of life in Fairlie not only include precious times of blessing from the Lord, but also the lovely friendships that developed over that time.

On one occasion Mary and I were driving back to Fairlie from Invercargill where I had been sharing the word of the Lord. As we drove many miles in comfortable silence I became aware of something the Holy Spirit wanted me to share with the elders. I do not recall the specific matter that it applied to, but this statement is always worth keeping in mind. I told them that the only issue to concern themselves about was the question, "Is it God, or is it not?"

How often church leaders make decisions on the basis of whether something is suitable to their church culture, whether it has been successfully done elsewhere, whether people will understand it, whether the result of the action is obvious or not, whether it is compatible with their comfort zone, and whether most of the church members will agree to it once it has been explained to them. How much wiser to decide on the basis whether it is God or not, and to tell the people how the Holy Spirit made it plain to us.

Well prior to one Easter we chatted about doing something 'special' over that weekend. Because Fairlie folk are ever so hospitable it was felt that each family should consider inviting folk from elsewhere to come and spend the weekend with them. Programme? We decided that, nearer the time, those of us who became aware of something we should do would make it known to others. The idea was that we would participate in whatever we felt was for us.

As an example, I mentioned that one thing I really warmed to was to start the weekend by worshipping the Lord early on Friday morning. Murray Bell immediately told us that that was exactly what he wanted, and asked me if we would go out to the farm and join with them in magnifying the Lord together. Many others joined in. On the Adams farm that day there was a barbecue lunch with a whole crowd participating.

Over the weekend, folk joined in various such events, all the time being aware of sharing at a spiritual level, and honouring the Lord in everything.

Another morning, folk returned to Murray's place to praise and worship the Lord. Murray shared that the previous day he had spent considerable time sitting down by the river. As a result of that quiet meditation he had something to share with us. He seemed to find it difficult, and so I asked, "Murray, is it the building?"

This referred to the old dark and dingy ex-cinema that the fellowship used. This was what Murray had to share. Gradually everyone heard from the Lord for themselves that it was no longer to be used. I commented that it seemed to me that the one-man pastor leadership function and the ownership of church buildings have been two of the greatest problems in church life over the past several centuries. Who could deny it?

In my book *Revelatory Adventure* I wrote the following few paragraphs about major changes that had taken place in Fairlie over the years we were involved there. Allan Bell, who is in heaven now, repeatedly told folk that these things came about because of the grace of God in and through my life. The credit is the Lord's alone.

From *Revelatory Adventure*—

"Throughout New Zealand there are now many, many Christians who identify with the lifestyle described in this book. To be specific, I will comment on the group of believers who have been our home fellowship over recent years.

"The time came when there was unanimous agreement that the Holy Spirit was calling the Fellowship beyond decentralisation to a full disbanding of its structure. This involved an acceptance that there would be no further gatherings except when there was a calling together by the Lord for a specific purpose. It also meant getting rid of the building the fellowship owned, and the closing of its bank account.

"Over the several years since the fellowship disbanded, the Christians there have continued to enjoy fellowship with Jesus; indeed, more so than before. Realising that they must look to Him and not to men, drawing on His grace rather than relying on the sup-

port of a church system, has increased maturity and enhanced godliness.

"These believers haven't backslidden or become worldly. They are joyfully accepting opportunities to share Jesus with unbelievers. They comment, that now the fellowship no longer exists, people who don't know the Lord seem far more friendly and open to listen to the good news of Christ's love

"With them, we, too, are conscious of being imperfect and inadequate, yet are looking to the Lord Jesus for sufficient understanding so that we may be what He wants us to be right where we are. In these believers there is an honest desire to learn the way of the Lord more perfectly and to see Him wonderfully glorified in the whole area about them."

Over ten years have passed since *Revelatory Adventure* was published. In Fairlie, with a population of less than 900, there is today a quite vibrant community of believers operating solely under the Lordship of Jesus and doing everything you would expect from a structured church, except wasting time, effort and resources on maintaining a system and a structure.

During these years there have been over 30 folk who have experienced salvation in Christ, and a similar number of baptisms. This compares more than favourably with a similar time period prior to the man made church 'structure' coming to an end. There has been loving care of those with need of some kind, as well as seasons of earnest combined prayer for the town, the needs of children from Christian families being provided for, and unbelievers visited in their homes with offers of help and prayer. There has often been delightful spontaneity as well as refreshing variety in believers coming together for some Spirit-revealed purpose or other.

Our eventual departure from Fairlie came about because for many years Mary had had a vision of our living overlooking water, and had longed to see it come about. This resulted in several delightful years living in Diamond Harbour which is not far from Christchurch.

I am grateful to Neil Riley, who visits Fairlie from time to time, for helping me with these insights into the current situation there.

A God-filled Nobody

Part 4

Africa

A God-filled Nobody

N THE LATE 1970S WE ATTENDED A RENEWAL conference being held at the Tauranga racecourse. There we met an Australian, Gerald Rowlings, who had recently been involved with missionary work at White River in the Eastern Transvaal province of South Africa. With other leaders we were staying at Faith Bible College enjoying delightful fellowship as we shared meals together before going in to the meetings. This brother, who had not heard me speak in a meeting, told me very earnestly that he believed that God wanted me in South Africa at that time.

I told him that I would be sensitive to the Holy Spirit in that regard, knowing that, if it was the 'now' word of the Lord for me, an inner conviction about it would grow in my heart. We should not accept something as the word of God to us simply because someone declares that it is. In the final analysis, only the Holy Spirit within us can declare that.

Not long after that, Dick Mills from the USA was speaking in Ngaruawahia which is not far from Hamilton, where we were living. With some other friends we went out to one of Dick's meetings. We sat well back in the church, and I deliberately tried to remain somewhat hidden. However, Dick soon saw me and called out, "Is that John Beaumont back there?" Others told him it was and he either spoke to me or about me, basically saying that the Lord would soon have me travelling to other countries to share God's word.

Some days later the Hamilton Elim church pastor, Les Covic, whom I had known for many years, spoke to me. "Do you know Dick Mills told us that God has a worldwide ministry for you?" he inquired. He proceeded to tell me that he, Les, had chatted with a number of mature believers we both knew, and they all agreed with that assessment. I have always been very cautious about someone declaring a worldwide ministry for anyone else.

Some time later I was down in the New Zealand capital of Wellington, speaking for several days at the Mirimar Baptist Church, where a beloved friend, Eric Chambers, was the minister at that time. I mentioned the things I have shared above with Eric and he told me that I had better pack my bags. I told him that all of this may simply be God's way of calling me to focus intercessory prayer on South Africa and the several countries that were now being mentioned.

Eric's last word on the subject: "You'll never get away with it!"

I submitted the matter to three brothers in the Lord in Hamilton with whom we had a delightfully close spiritual relationship. I valued their interest, advice and prayer support. Each week, with our wives we had lunch together in one or the other's homes. We guys would usually get together the same evening to chat and pray. A conviction grew in my heart that I must venture forth.

In special ways the Lord provided for the cost of our travel – and not through those guys, either. Mary and I have always loved Hudson Taylor's observation "God's work done in God's way never lacks God's supply." From that time on we have not asked anyone for money, nor even told anybody that we were 'living by faith'.

We abhor the thought of sending out heart-tugging letters, let alone glossy magazines, with pleas for financial support for some so-called 'faith work' or other. I simply settled it with the Lord that since this was His idea, then it was His responsibility to supply everything necessary for it. If supply stopped, then I would know that a season had ended and happily move into whatever life-style change He indicated. I also expressed to Him my purpose not to journey one mile more than He directed.

Our First Visit

AND SO WE SET OUT ON A JOURNEY THAT basically involved a month in South Africa, a month in England and a month in the USA, although we did minister in several meetings in Brisbane, Sydney, and Perth, Australia, on our way to South Africa.

On another visit to Australia we attended a gathering in a packed-out Sydney Town Hall. These were the days when the Charismatic Movement was very widespread and active in our part of the world. Many mature and godly believers participated. Christians from many different churches would gather together for special celebration services, worshipping the Lord together.

Who would have thought it? I had been invited to be the main speaker for the occasion! I remember that there were probably 15 or 20 ministers and priests on the huge platform. Amazingly I was so relaxed, and even enjoying myself so much, that, as I spoke to that large gathering I joked that the line of men behind me needed what I was saying more than all the folk in front of me.

I'll never forget it! People stood up all across the building, clapping and cheering. These were their own pastors and priests! I turned around and warmly greeted each of those men. There was a unique 'something' about this occasion that has given it a special place in my memory.

The flight from Perth to Johannesburg, which stopped briefly at Mauritius for refuelling, took about fourteen hours. When you add the airport time involved at both ends of an international flight, plus the jet lag involved in a ten-hour time difference between NZ and SA, you may understand how weary we were the Saturday forenoon that we arrived.

That evening I spoke with joyful anointing at a Full Gospel Businessmen's meeting in a large hall that our host, Brother Willie Roelands, had built on his lovely 'El Dorado' property outside Johannesburg. It was a privilege to be in that great nation at the clear direction of the Lord.

The next morning we were picked up and taken to the Church on the Move across the city, where I was to speak. I recall the words of the pastor, Reg Bendixen, as he drew the service to a close. "We have not heard a sermon this morning," he told the worshippers, "We have had an encounter with the truth." Hopefully he was not simply referring to a truth or truths but, "the Truth."

I was taken to one of their homes and brought back to the centre for the evening service. I was so 'bushed' by then my legs felt rubbery. It was only later that we learned the significance of that day for a group of the younger men there who had been praying earnestly prior to our visit that this would be the beginning of a new day for that church.

After involvement in other gatherings, including with brother Jacobs and his 'coloured' church, Mary and I took a train down to Durban in Natal. I was dismayed to learn that during our ten days there I was scheduled to speak in twenty-seven gatherings. To me that was absolutely ridiculous—I am not a talking machine! Lamentably we live in a generation of words, words, and more words. I recall on one occasion joking with pastors in America that you can always tell when some one is in Babylon—they babble on.

There were home meetings, men's meetings, luncheon meetings, a service in a thriving Indian

church and I do not recall what else! I do remembering speaking to groups as diverse as FGBMFI, Ro-
man Catholic, Presbyterian, Church of England and
Assembly of God. I felt shatteringly exhausted after
those ten days when we flew down to Cape Town.

Our gracious hosts while we were in Durban were
John and Jean Alcock who were going through a period of difficult business circumstances and yet were
kindness personified. Their home was in beautiful
Kloof, inland a little. With a sub-tropical climate, flow-
ering shrubs and trees seemed to be everywhere.
These delightful people became life-long friends
as we returned to stay with them on later visits to
South Africa.

In Cape Town we were met at the airport by a
colonel Eddie McCullam, who was the military commander of the historic fortified 'castle' in the city. Eddie and Peggy were caring people. He was president
of the local FGBMFI chapter. Thankfully there were
not many meetings arranged for us and so I told
Eddie that we were exhausted and would get away
alone for a few days to recuperate after the Durban
speaking marathon.

We moved into an apartment at the beautiful seaside resort of Seapoint. Strolling along the waterfront in the sunshine, looking at the delightful flowers, and observing people around us was all very pleasant, as was not even needing to converse with well-meaning people, far less speak at meetings.

Back in Johannesburg, three couples took us down to the Eastern Transvaal, to the Kruger National Park for a few days. Our fellowship together was really delightful, and viewing such a variety of animals and birds in their natural habitat was enthralling. We stopped our cars at a spot on the road where others cars had stopped.

Well back from the road some lions were lying in the grass, but it was almost impossible to see them. Reg got out of his car, walked to the one we were in, and said that his motor had stalled and wouldn't restart. Happily there were jumper leads in one of the cars. I said that I would help, and jumped out of the car, helped lift the bonnets and attach the jumper leads. The car started immediately and we returned to our cars. People along the line had been shouting, "Get back into your cars, get back into your cars."

We did what had to be done and were no worse off for it though a couple of lions had lifted their heads to look at us. On the last morning one of the men prayed, "And let John see a lion today, Lord." He wanted me to get a good clear sight of this 'king of the beasts'. I added, "Yes, Lord, on the road please." That brought smiles and a chuckle or two. Later on we turned a corner in the road on the way out of the park to see a lion walking leisurely along the road. Apparently this was quite unusual. We returned to the Kruger on a subsequent visit to South Africa.

A Unique Opportunity

TOWARDS THE END OF THAT ACTION filled month, which entailed a sharp learning curve for me, we were provided with an outstanding opportunity, thanks in the main to brother Reg Bendixen, a man I sincerely loved. Reg passed on to me an invitation to speak each day at a gathering of pastors and delegates from Assemblies of God throughout southern Africa. I will mention without elaborating that this denomination was formed in South Africa, probably a century ago by now. Differences were sufficient for the International Assemblies of God to have their own mission work in South Africa.

Reg told me that no 'outsider' had ever been asked to speak at these conferences, which were held once every two years. Usually different AOG pastors were given the honour of addressing the conference only once during the week, and yet I was invited to speak each day. Someone told me that there were about 900 white delegates there and about 1500 Africans.

That there were hungry and earnest men present

can be seen in the fact that during that week many of them invited me to visit their local assembly. Although most delegates could understand English perfectly well, an interpreter was used for those who could not. Some preachers struggle to speak through an interpreter, acting as if they don't enjoy being interrupted, and looking at and talking to the interpreter all the time.

Thankfully this has not been a problem to me as I have shared the word of the Lord with the listeners. The interpreter was exceptional. I told the gathering that I had given him freedom to share the flow of my heart even if the translation was not word for word exact. During one message I stopped for a moment and asked, "Help me Lord." Instead of interpreting that, he responded, "Me too Lord!" It was lovely.

If anyone had asked if God had manifested Himself at that conference in any special way, I am confident that everyone would have pointed to one particular morning session. Throughout the previous night the Holy Spirit had responded to the cries of my heart, touched me very deeply during those sacred hours, and filled my whole being with both a flood-tide of divine grace and a very deep awareness of God's presence.

When I stood silently for a moment before speaking, a holy hush settled on the entire congregation. I have no idea what was shared, but I vividly recollect that people absorbed and reacted to what was shared as if they were hearing directly from God Himself.

Nowadays the word 'awesome' has been cheapened abominably, when perhaps it should always have been reserved for the Almighty. That morning was really and truly awesome. No altar call or invitation of any kind was given but the Superintendent of the church made his way forward and fell on his knees weeping. Many others responded to God in similar fashion.

The next day at breakfast the Superintendent spoke of the gathering asking me, "You wouldn't call that prophecy, would you?" He meant that they believed in the exercise of such a ministry, but my sharing hadn't met their traditional norms. What did it matter? I simply told him that many in New Zealand would, and left it at that. Our prayer was, as always, that this time of special revelation and grace would result in continuing enhancement of Christian character in the men, further equipage in the Spirit for their ministry and a showing forth of God's glory in His church.

Johannesburg

OW I WILL NO LONGER FOLLOW chronological order but share from our experiences over quite a period of years. We have returned again and again to this country that we rapidly grew to love deeply. It will always have a special place in my heart. Let me mention that although we have travelled far and wide around the world, our travel has not always been rapid, or 'whistle-stop' as our American friends say. Apart from in the United States we have often stayed for three months, six months or even a year or more in one particular place where we mainly related to one local church situation.

Uncle Willie and his wife Hannah, both of whom are in heaven now, were always lovingly hospitable. I recall speaking at an FGBMFI dinner that had been arranged by Uncle Willie, the South African president. Before the dinner started I had been told that they had booked that lovely dining hall at the central railway station for a certain time and had to vacate it right after that. Phil and Vicki Wassung were there that night, as well as Phil's brother and sister-in-law.

A God-filled Nobody

After the dinner several committee members and friends addressed the gathering, so that when I was invited to bring the main message of the evening it was almost time for everyone to leave. Accordingly, with respect to what I had been told, I simply reminded everyone that they had heard some lovely and important things that evening, wished them God's blessing, and sat down.

A similar thing happened at a lunch meeting I addressed some time later, after which Uncle Willie told me that he had advised various presidents around the country that I was unpredictable, but very worthwhile having at their chapters. Of course I pointed out to him that at this point I was totally predictable, and would always honour whatever time restrictions were placed on me.

I may add that at a Sunday morning church service in New Zealand I was once allocated fourteen minutes. At a large Church of England service in Britain I was allocated eighteen minutes. In other places I have been told to finish at a very specific time. None of this has bothered me because I have realized that I am only responsible for whatever time I am given. But I have always let the congregation know the situation, such as starting a message with, "In the eighteen minutes allocated to me . . . " I have sometimes wondered whether a leader here or there has been given a 'bit of stick' over having imposed such a restriction.

The second time we came to South Africa I had agreed to pastor a local church in Johannesburg for six months, with that time able to be extended if both the elders and I agreed to do that. The pastor and his wife were going to be out of the country for six months. He told me that when he returned he was going to take up travelling evangelistic work.

In that fellowship our hearts and lives became entwined with brothers and sisters who are still precious to us today. Among these are Ron and Marcelle Saxby and Guy and Jackie Dennison. I hasten to add to this list Phil and Vicky Wassung. Even though they were not members of that church they are very precious friends. Others we lovingly remember are Guido [in heaven now] and Irene Willems, Winton and Ingrid Van der Merwe, Owen and Patsy Hughes, Sheila Holdsworth and Cecil Ravenscroft.

On a later visit we made to South Africa Ronnie

arranged some combined special meetings. I was one of two speakers, and I liked that kind of balance. When the other speaker and myself were chatting alone during the midday break, he told me something of himself, including being involved with visits of Derek Prince and such men to South Africa for special conventions. My co-speaker had been declared an apostle at that time. We discussed the servant role that is implicit and essential in every ministry and function in the church.

After considerable pleasant conversation I asked, "What will you do when the people want a king?" "No, no brother," he protested, "I don't want that." I told him that people would, though, and left it at that. Certain involvement I had with that brother later on gave indication to me that he had acquiesced to the people's wishes. So many do, to everyone's detriment.

Things that seem very minor sometimes get stuck in one's memory somehow. Mary and I went to a restaurant in Johannesburg for a meal one evening. I asked the young waitress if she was a student, and found that she was. When I tipped her I gave her more than the meal cost. She started to cry and hurried back to the kitchen area.

After a while she came back and asked, "Was the money you gave me to pay for your meals?" We told her that we had once been students and enjoyed the opportunity to give her that and to wish her God's blessing on her life. She could scarcely contain her gratitude. Responding to the Holy Spirit in simple and ordinary events of daily living is fulfiling and enjoyable, isn't it?

Sharing the lives of lovely families was a special privilege for us in Johannesburg. On numerous occasions we enjoyed the camaraderie of relaxed barbecues [braai, they call them] and from time to time went away with these folk for a weekend together, or at times longer. The blending of enjoyable informality, family life, and serious discussion, along with a lovely awareness of the Lord in the midst will long be remembered. Precious memories indeed!

Over the years we have observed some of these youngsters grow and develop from infancy right through to young adulthood. The Scriptures record that "Jesus increased in wisdom and stature, and in favour with God and man." We have shared a little of the parents' pride as their children have not only developed in their academic and social skills, but even more importantly, have matured into fine young Christians. We love them all.

For one weekend away with a fellowship Mary [mainly] and I took responsibility for preparing meals for everyone and supervising serving them. It really is fun to serve, isn't it? When we first arrived at the retreat site the manager of the place took us aside and showed us a supply of anti-snake serum in the refrigerator.

A day or two before a deadly cobra had been killed in a toilet block. We learned that it is normal for the mate of these snakes to come looking for its partner. We were shown where the snake had come from, and took good care to steer everyone away from that area. In New Zealand, as in Ireland we have no snakes and this causes us to be particularly cautious of them.

A believer in Johanesburg invited me to have lunch with him at the Wanderers Sports Club. It was pleasant to have this leisurely one-on-one chat with the brother. At the start of the meal he said, "I drink wine." I replied, "I see.' A little later he told me, "I drink whisky." Again I replied, "I see," and left it at that.

"You have nothing to say about it?" he inquired. I told him that he was answerable to God, not to me, and mentioned that I was going through a season of listening to the Living Bible on tape for a while each night when I went to bed. The night before I had heard from the Book of Proverbs, this statement: "A king shall not drink wine nor whisky." Amazing timing wasn't it? My only other comment was, "I gather that you may have little desire to 'reign in life by this one, Jesus Christ.'

When we have stayed in an area for any length of time Mary and I have often been provided with an apartment or some such accommodation. This has always been deeply appreciated. I am the kind of person who needs plenty of time alone, and Mary loves being a home-maker and having guests in for a meal now and again.

Over the years I became aware that when a family invited us for a meal the adults would be placed at one end of the dining table, and children at the other—or even at a separate table. While the adults chatted about the ways of the Lord, children tended to whisper among themselves. This makes one wonder whether the impression being given is that our kind of discussion is for adults only. That would be very unfortunate.

Accordingly we have encouraged placing children among the adults and bringing them into the conversation. It doesn't matter whether they are South Africans, Irish, Americans or New Zealanders, I have enjoyed asking children, "What has God said to you lately?" Now that could easily embarrass an adult, but Christian children love to share something they have recently heard. I love it too!

Bloemfontein

RONNIE, GUY, WINTON VAN DER MERWE and I drove from Johannesburg for a weekend with 'coloured' folk in Bloemfontein. Coloured folk I had been involved with in Cape Town had arranged it with Willie Norris, in whose home we stayed. When we stopped for refreshments along the way one of the men commented that this was a new step for him—to be staying in the home of coloured people. I told them that I had no idea what we were coming to and we could be stepping back into the dark ages of churchdom. All I knew was that we were to be servants among them.

We were greeted warmly and provided with gracious hospitality. A sizable group of men gathered on an open verandah and under the shade of a nearby tree. After introductions, Willie asked me, "Now John, tell us why you have come here?" I replied that he knew why we had come—he had invited us because of what Cape Town brothers had told him. He was not to be put off, saying something like, "Yes, but you didn't have to accept the invitation. What is your purpose in coming?"

"Willie" I said, "all I can do is tell you what I told these men as we drove here. We came to be your servants." You should have heard—and seen—all those men laughing almost hilariously. As the laughter died down a little I asked why they had laughed that much. I know that the idea of whites serving coloureds may be somewhat strange, but Willie was bright enough to hold a high position in an insurance company with workers of different races under him.

Then we were told that various church leaders had visited them from different parts of the country. Some wanted them to join their group or denomination and others wanted them to come under their apostleship or oversight, but nobody before had chosen to serve them.

They had been alert to sense the inevitable dangers of human control, the demands for conformity and the domination that are all inherent in denominationalism.

Willie told us how he had found the Saviour through the sovereign grace of God. He then thought that he should buy a Bible, and did so. Following that he thought he had better try another new experience and go to church. He didn't like it a bit, but thought he must have hit on a 'dud' and tried another church. After attending several more churches he was a little perplexed. Why did none of these places feel right for him?

He visited a relative, brother-in-law I think, and even though his relative didn't know the Lord Jesus he told him of his dilemma. The brother-in-law's neighbour was also there. He told of his conversion, and the wonderful difference it had made for him to personally experience God's love. What happened next? The two men yielded their lives to Christ, trusting him for personal salvation. Several others that he told also came to the Lord.

Willie had a bright idea. They had no need to go to church now, they could be church themselves. The thrilling story is that they considered themselves to be Gospel messengers, telling other non-believers about salvation in Christ.

The next day we walked along the road with Willie and his family towards a hall they had hired for the occasion. I doubt if I had ever seen anything like it before.

People came out to the front of their properties to greet them. Some called Willie over for a moment or two's chat, and others joined in the cheerful stroll down the road. Not only was the meeting room filled, but as Willie told us about several other similar groups who were meeting in different directions some miles apart. Several thousand in all, I believe, all of them having received the word of the Lord through these gospel messengers. Wonderful!

As a prelude to my speaking at any stage of the weekend I had told the men with me that if they knew they had the right word to share at any precise moment while I was speaking, then to step forward and I would yield to them. At Willie's home the previous afternoon it went well. After a while Willie enthusiastically said he would like to join in as he felt led by the Holy Spirit. It was all very refreshing and really alive.

As we sat there that pleasant afternoon I pointed to a garden hose that lay on the grass close by. "That's what God wants you to be," I told them, "A hose pipe through which the waters of life can flow." They saw the importance of being firmly attached to the main water supply, and having no 'switch off' blockage mechanism at their end of it. This simple picture seemed to catch their imagination.

At the Sunday morning gathering the things I shared were translated into Afrikaans, the predominant language there. At the back, groups sat on the floor around several different individuals who quietly translated into other African languages. As at the house the previous day, there were several times when I stood back as one or other of the guys carried on with sharing the word of the Lord.

Towards the end Winton Van der Merwe began to share, and I suggested he speak in Afrikaans, his first language. I knew the people would really appreciate that, and I had no need to understand what was said.

When he sat down I mentioned that there was one other thing to briefly add, and so I did. Winton had been about to share 'one more thing' but suddenly felt that he should not, so the congregation knew that I was following on exactly from Winton, without knowing a thing he had said.

This was seen as confirmation that our message had been truly received from God and we had simply been the conduits for it to reach them. Everyone blessed the Lord for His goodness, and we returned to Johannesburg confident that the brothers and sisters we had met in those days had been encouraged and blessed by the God of their salvation.

Durban

WE HAVE BEEN INVOLVED IN NUMEROUS gatherings around Natal, mostly in the Durban and Pinetown areas.

I was scheduled to speak at a meeting of combined churches one evening, with the delightful arrangement that I would meet with their leaders in the morning. I have always appreciated opportunities to speak to such men, both individually and corporately.

It is a privilege to get alongside such people to encourage and bless them. I recall speaking at a ministers' fraternal in Invercargill, New Zealand, telling them that I had a love-hate attitude to leadership groups. "You all want to put on an air of godliness and success," I told them, "Whereas I have been vice-president of the strugglers' club." It was my joking kind of way to challenge them to honesty and reality. I had some interesting chats afterwards! The subject that had been allocated to me that day was, 'Ministering in a Generation Seeking Renewal.'

I asked the Natal leaders for forgiveness since I

was a bit weepy that morning, but I had been on my face before the Lord that night, with Gorbachev deeply impressed on my heart. From the other side of the room a precious Zulu brother, Emanuel, who was to be my interpreter that night, jumped to his feet, ran over and hugged me exclaiming, "Me too, brother." It was quite a moving moment.

This was at a time when Gorbachev was to make an historic visit to America. Perestroika and glasnost had not come to the fore at that time. One of the preachers, probably kicking in with some doctrinal prejudice asked, "You don't mean he is going to be converted, do you?" My reply was something like, "No, but he is going to see a new way forward for the leadership of his country."

As I thought about this matter the next day, I realized the Holy Spirit may very well have prompted pray-ers around the world to intercede for that man at that time. I marvelled at the way He can move in a realm unseen by the natural eye to orchestrate a spiritual activity in the body of Christ. It seems to me that natural man in his religiosity feels a need to organize and structure God's people far more than is necessary, healthy or right.

I recall another leadership group down in that area

that I joined for a day's retreat. The morning session commenced with a delightful period of praising and worshipping the Lord of all, who alone is worthy. It was sensitive, fragrant, and undoubtedly pleasing to the Lord. As the leader that day stood up to introduce me an elder called out, "Did you see all those demons fly out of here as we worshipped the Lord?"

When I stood to speak I addressed that brother saying, "I have a question for you. How did those demons get in here in the first place?" After all we were meeting in a leader's home! People do say foolish things at times, don't they? The initial questioner asked me how soon could I return to New Zealand! Over all I thoroughly enjoyed the day.

Over the years I have been asked whether I belong to such-and-such a group, organisation or movement. I may or may not have at some stages in my life, but over many years now my answer has been, "No, I am part of the moving of God." Surely, as soon as something is described as a movement, men have set boundaries to the purposes of God.

Reg Bendixon once told me of someone translating the Bible into an African language. Although they searched diligently there seemed to be no word for 'eternity' until one day a national rushed into the translator excitedly saying, "I have found it, I have found it." Eternity was translated into words literally meaning, "Life without boundaries."

When we are alive in the Spirit, and controlled by Him, we are 'people of the horizon' aren't we, where earth and heaven, time and eternity merge to some degree or other? Surely a fading out of man-made boundaries should ensue from such a walk.

A somewhat learned Presbyterian Minister in Durban once told me, "I have sorted out in my mind what you are. You are an evangelical mystic after the order of Tozer." I have definitely been described in far worse terms than that. It was a nice 'box', but still a box created from human reasoning. I would rather see myself as a servant of the Lord, a worshipper, a learner and a beginner.

Cape Town

WE PARTICIPATED IN A VARIETY OF meetings in the Cape Province. On one of our first visits to Cape Town I had the privilege of speaking in several combined Anglican services, and since then have also spoken in Assemblies of God, Presbyterian churches, a Methodist church, house churches and the like.

One satisfying aspect of our visits to Cape Town was a continuing involvement in John Langford's life and ministry. Over the years John and Jenny have been excellent friends. It has been very gratifying to observe a brother, growing, maturing and developing over the years. He and I have chatted, prayed and laughed together many a time as we have travelled to services, leaders' meetings and special gatherings. John had a lovely relationship with quite a number of coloured folk and I always enjoyed being involved in that.

The minister of a large Presbyterian church invited me to speak to a Cape Town Presbyterian ministers' fraternal. Naturally, I arrived there quite early, wanting to 'get the lay of the land'. As the minister and I chatted together in his office he said, "You seem to be a very radical man, Mr. Beaumont so let me ask you, what do you think is the future of the church?"

I asked whether he meant the local church he was involved with, his denomination, or the church worldwide. He suggested that I start with the local church right there. How grateful I am that the Holy Spirit has taught me over the years to be sensitive to His promptings as a way of life, and especially at a time like that. After a pause I told him the future of that church was not important since in was already irrelevant to the purposes of God. "Irrelevant," he said, "God told me that over a year ago." The fraternal gathering was wonderfully anointed and blessed of God.

I am happy to be considered radical if, as indicated in the word "radish" for example, it means to want to get to the root and or go back to the roots of Christianity. There is always a need to be challenged to "Return to the simplicity that there is in Christ."

Let me make very clear however, that in visiting any local 'work' all I wanted to receive from the Lord, and pass on to the hearers, was what God purposed to be the next step forward for them, and to encourage them in that. Before that though, would be a desire to encourage every believer to embark on a walk in the fullness of God's wonderful provision for them. It is a magnificent quest to seek to magnify the Lord in our thoughts, attitudes and behaviour day by day until it becomes a habit of daily life.

A Similar Question

ONE TIME IN A LEADERS' MEETING IN America I was asked a similar question about the future of the church. I sat silently for a minute or so, prompting the questioner to ask whether I could answer the question or not. "Of course I can" I replied, "I was just waiting for the answer so that I could pass it on to you." I proceeded to say that to understand the church of the future they should look back a hundred and more years.

In early America, which was much more rural then than now, people worked strenuously for long hours, day after day. They had to get wood chopped for the winter, fields ploughed and planted and then crops gathered in. They had often needed to tend cattle and other animals as well, perhaps, also hunting and shooting deer and the like to provide food for the bleak days of winter. For many it was normal to work from dawn to dusk.

In many situations a travelling preacher came around occasionally—perhaps only two or three times a year. There wasn't the time to attend prayer meetings, youth meetings, women's meetings and all the other meetings in today's church. However they could always find time to help get in the crops of some neighbour who had been injured, help preserve the fruit and vegetables for a neighbour whose wife had died, even if they lived some miles away.

For many this was a demonstration of their living faith. When they could gather together for some kind of special service one can imagine the freshness, joyful eagerness and reality in such a gathering. Americans can view their past with sentimental attachment, and so such a thought was relevant for them.

Back to Cape Town

JOHN LANGFORD DROVE ME BACK TO CAPE Town from the Eastern Cape. Someone there had presented a somewhat unusual and self-serving prayer request to us. It was from their dad who owned a vineyard that wasn't far off our route. Would we swing by his place and pray for rain in that area, since another week or so without would mean the loss of an entire year's harvest. I made no promises. As we drove near I said to John something like, "I am too tired to visit those people, so I'll trust for rain for them here and now."

When we arrived back in Cape Town Mary and I became involved in a series of meetings with the Wynburg Presbyterian church. The minister, Angus Bain, was a long time friend of Stan Firth. I understand that they attended college together in Scotland. One evening, when we arrived someone told us that a package had arrived for us. It was a carton containing twelve large bottles of excellent grape juice. It must have rained!

One evening I became concerned about a young

woman in the service whose dad was an elder, and passed on a word of encouragement and gentle urging from the Lord. Several years later I was invited back to speak at the church, and also at a church camp. There was a different minister there then. That elder dad, a big Afrikaaner, came out to greet me with a huge smile and a big hug. He was grateful for the day we had been involved in his daughter turning a spiritual corner.

At the camp the daughter was part of the music group involved with their worship sessions. I was unwell at the time and found the vibration of instruments quite distressing. Accordingly I asked forgiveness and walked about outside for that part of the meetings. However, that daughter talked about it with Mary. With remarkable humility and in a gracious spirit of love she and the other musicians laid their instruments aside so that I could remain in the meetings. I cannot express just how much I appreciated this thoughtfulness. It was certainly 'going the second mile'.

At that camp a couple asked us to see their two little children. Although I cannot remember the occasion, they told us that when we had first come to the

Wynburg church they had asked me to pray about their inability to have children. There are times when I know I must take a different approach, but in that case I was able to pray with confidence and assurance. They were showing us the answer to prayer.

There are times when believers fall into a trap of thinking, "If only . . . then I could live a triumphant God-glorifying Christian life. The 'if only' includes such things as finding a marriage partner, having children, having better health, one's spouse being more loving, having sufficient funds to cover extra expenses, and so on, and so on. How blessed are those who learn early in life [or perhaps learn at any stage of life] that fulfilment is not found in altered circumstances and increased blessings. It is found in Christ alone so that we can experientially know the reality of peace like a river, and joy unspeakable and full of glory, regardless of circumstances. Amazing grace!

Before moving north from South Africa I will make a couple of observations and then briefly share three strange questions that I have been asked in various situations there.

South Africa is a very large country with huge varieties of race, culture, scenery and climate. The major cities of Johannesburg, Cape Town, Durban, Pretoria and Bloemfontein are very different from each other, as are other cities too. Johannesburg has an elevation of 5,800 feet [that is, over 1,780 metres]. Durban and Cape Town are close to sea level.

We were deeply appreciative of the opportunity to visit South Africa the first time. Our love for this nation of great potential has increased and grown over the years. It has a special place in our hearts.

The first question is "Can a woman be an elder?" My reply, "I thought women would be too smart to want to be." I suspect that the question is based on the officialdom placed upon what is intended to be a servant role.

The next question is, "Can a Christian have a demon?" My reply, "Why? How many do you want?" This was something of a hot potato in many circles in South Africa when we first went there. Valueless theological arguments do not appeal to me. I have often told people of my graduating from theological studies, and "By the grace of God recovering from it." Some never do.

The third question: "Are you an apostle?" This came from a group of leaders who liked to pigeon-hole everyone. More than that, once such a ministry is recognised and accepted, men are encouraged to act like what they are declared to be. My response was, "I have only come here to be God's servant among you. Sometimes when I leave a place people say, 'he is a prophet' at other places, 'he is an apostle' or 'he is a teacher'". I make no effort to be one thing or another, but rather set my heart to walk in an ongoing love relationship with the Lord Jesus and respond to the Holy Spirit whatever His prompting may be. I am glad that God has changed my role from time to time over the years.

Although I understand and appreciate these ministries which God has given to His church, I suspect that many leaders suffer from 'hardening of the categories.' I am content to be a worshipper and a servant. For what it is worth, my personal observation has led me to believe that almost without exception the formal recognition of even God-given ministries results in a sub-standard and mediocre expression of them. Jesus, build your church!

It amuses me somewhat to see the awe in which

Christians hold preachers who are described as "great Bible teachers" when that statement itself is not a Bible term! We are called to teach life, to teach truth, to teach Christ.

When I told Ronnie and Marcelle Saxby of my writing about the grace of God, including our visits to South Africa, Ronnie sent back these comments:

"The grace of God . . . the more you experience, the greater the depth there is still to plumb.

"Irrespective of one's maturity in God, new revelations of His grace are always fresh, energising and inspirational. They are timely interventions to encourage, sustain and infuse life.

"I look back to my first meeting with John and Mary some time in 1978. I did not know it then but I was standing on the threshold of a new experience . . . the Grace of God that liberates from the law of suffocating Christian obligation. What an amazing vista . . . what an amazing journey . . .

"I can remember taking months . . . many months to assimilate and walk in the depth of this grace ministered to us. Today I am still challenged by John's

161

presence and the grace of God that is imparted in heartfelt fellowship and love.

"There is so much more to see . . . "

Zimbabwe

W E WELL REMEMBER THE FIRST TIME we flew from Johannesburg to Salisbury that is now named Harare, the capital of Zimbabwe. A short time before a Viscount passenger plane had been shot down over Zimbabwe with the loss of everyone on board. So our plane flew high until it was time to descend rapidly to the airport.

The pilot announced that the terminal building was safe, but terrorists were in control at the end of the runway where the plane would touch down. Since it was evening we were told to keep our blinds closed until the plane reached the terminal. It was important not to let any light shine out. We didn't!

I have long since learned that not everybody listens to announcements on planes. I don't always, myself. As soon as we touched down the man at the window in the row in front of us lifted his blind full up. There is no prize for guessing how quickly I reached right over and pulled that blind right down again. Otherwise it might have been "curtains" for us.

Zimbabwe is a delightful country with lovely scenery, superb climate and precious people. It has been a very wealthy nation but today is virtually bank-rupt. They are in danger of serious human tragedy because of a grave lack of life's basic necessities. It has suffered through a common African idea of democracy, which is "One man, one vote, once."

Over the years since so-called independence many thousands have suffered and died at the hands cruel men; blacks at the hand of blacks more than anyone else. May God hasten a day of peace, plenty and true freedom to these needy people, and may their present anguish and suffering somehow bring them into a vital, living relationship with the Lord Jesus Christ, who is their one true Hope.

On that first visit we were taken to speak at a church in a small town some distance from Harare. It was somewhat interesting to see the men wearing side-arms, but quite rivetting to see a little old lady come into the row in front of where we initially sat. She nonchalantly stacked her machine gun against the end of the pew!

The church service was followed by lunch as often happens in rural areas anywhere. A farmer, whom we have come to know very well since then, invited us to go with our hosts to his farm afterwards. When we piled into our vehicles a fine looking young man came across and said to John Lenton, "I will go first." He wouldn't have it otherwise and so it was. The road was interesting. For some miles it was simply two narrow strips of concrete or tarmac that the wheels ran on. Nowadays these sealed strips have become very broken up along the edges making driving on them quite difficult. A car has to move off the side of the strips to pass another car. This causes a lot of damage to tyres because of the broken edges that are quite deep.

Do you know why that young man insisted on driving ahead? It was because on more than one occasion cars had been blown up by terrorists who could easily dig into the clay and insert a pressure bomb under the concrete. He was risking his life to make sure that we were safe.

The last time I was in Zimbabwe, someone told me that several of the folk who have become good friends over the years since that time were touched and transformed by the grace of God at that service.

I have no recollection of it, but someone told me that I had spoken to [or about, perhaps] a brother on one of our visits who was battling over being baptized. My statement had been, apparently, "If you won't go to the river, the river will come to you." It happened, so I was told. The river overflowed until his house was awash with it. My emphasis over many years now has been on the work of God in man's inner being rather than external things, so it is a little surprising that I said such a thing. Mind you, I have baptized a number of people in that country.

Nancy Fraser was one of the first Zimbabweans we met because we went there initially at the invitation of Intercessors for Zimbabwe, and she, with Iris Wassung, Phil's mother who is in heaven now, was involved with that group. On another occasion John Langford and Phil came with me to an Intercessors retreat. The facilities were fine and the fellowship great.

I urged the locals to have the courage to question, and if necessary or wise, to discard, customs and procedures that had been imparted by the western church and may not now be suitable for their culture in independent Zimbabwe. We were thrilled with the number of these beloved nationals who came to chat with us in our chalet.

They had been delighted to hear the things we had shared, even though one or two foreign missionaries were a little shaken by it. Surely, in any and every situation believers need to be living out the reality of lives that are "hid with Christ in God." It is His Lordship that is vital in our lives rather than conformity to man-made procedures, customs and rules.

The old saying, "In essentials unity, in non-essentials liberty, in all things charity" is great as long as we refuse to allow form and structure to be considered essential. As I told a pastor in New Zealand, "Some hold on to what should be let go, and let go what should be held on to."

On one of our visits we stayed out on the farm John and Cicely Lenton were managing. No special gatherings had been arranged, but friends had been told that we were there. By the numbers who came out to see us, our being there must certainly have been 'noised abroad.' We sat around sharing together the goodness of God and His present desires for His people. At times we strolled around outside, and at times I sneaked away to our bedroom for a rest. Some nights people slept on couches and even on the floor.

A God-filled Nobody

One day a group of Pastors came out from Harare to chat with me. When John Lenton got up to leave the room I urged him to stay in and enjoy the afternoon with us. The pastors fired some questions at me, and I did my best to answer them. I am well aware of the weariness that pressures can bring to such men, as well as the temptations they face. In my years in pastoral ministry I came to see that this is a man-made function in which we are expected to perform according to the church's expectations.

Accordingly, such men need an enormous supply of God's grace and continual encouragement from His people. It was a glad day of release for me when I told some of the leaders in a church I pastored that I could no longer be their traditional Baptist pastor. I wanted to fulfil the unique ministry that God had equipped me for, and to release them into their unique ministries as well. For a season it was great.

During that afternoon one of the pastors said to me, "You must be a threatened man." I understood him to be speaking of the provocative edge to my ministry and my willingness to obey the Lord even when it went against traditional norms. I told him that the opposite was true, and that they were the threatened men. I was a servant of the Lord owning nothing, controlling nothing, and heading up nothing. I was under no pressure to record, compare, tabulate and report visible and tangible success, or to obey men rather than God. Then I was no longer required there, and that was great too.

In contrast to that, they knew the competitiveness that creeps into ministry and the inward and external pressure for them to have a 'growing' church so that budgets could be met and salaries paid. Of course these things are usually couched more carefully in high-sounding spiritual terminology. Pity the pastors of sub-standard man-made churches.

Mind you, I have always shunned being a 'loner'. When I began ministering internationally, a group of mature Christian leaders in New Zealand, who were widely accepted and well recognised, served as a board of reference for me. I gladly sought their counsel and advice and shared my life and ministry with them, seeking their input. Later on we found it more effective to identify with groups in countries that I visited. Either way, there were brothers who could assure me whether or not I was hearing the Holy Spirit clearly and correctly.

When I submitted what I have written about Zimbabwe to Nancy Fraser she wrote back:

"I would like to see something added about the fruit of your visits to Zimbabwe. The South Side Fellowship where you spoke, and which was quite close to where I lived at the time, was going through a crisis. Because a large number of people had left this country, the congregations of the Bible Temple church and the Assembly of God came together, calling themselves the South Side Fellowship.

"A group of us caught hold of the truth you had been preaching, but the rest of the people were upset, wanting to remain exactly as they were. Rather than have contention 'brother with brother,' those of us who wanted to move on in our love walk with the Lord Jesus began meeting in a double garage. You had preached about a shaking taking place and we were eager to have the Holy Spirit shake off from us all that hindered His freedom to be God among us. Precious times at the Master's feet ensued for us.

At the Christian Life Centre you spoke about 'digging deep ditches of desire' and about seeking God for His revelation of 'the key' for every situation.

These two messages have often been brought to our remembrance over the years as the Lord has taken us on in our walk with Him. We have come to see that Christ is the key. It is "Christ in you, the hope of glory" that the Lord has shown us by revelation of Himself. This is to bring pleasure to the Father and to restore the testimony of Jesus to His people.

"That is the desire of our hearts. On your last visit you spoke of God's desire to settle down and feel completely 'at home' in us. We learnt a little song about that. Having laid hold of these truths, one is spoiled for anything less. We abandoned the man-made, man-controlled church system in 1980, and have never returned to it. Delightfully, the Lord continues to lead us on in our relationship with Himself.

"On a personal note, your ministry came to me when I was at the crossroads. Iris Wassung had been taken home to heaven, and I was burnt out. Through your sharing the Lord truly turned my life around. I came to recognize that I am accepted in the Beloved and that Father has a special place for me in His divine purposes. People described the change in me as a 'miracle' after my friend Rita and I came back *from our visit to the UK. That was the grace of God working through you.*

"Zimbabwe is in deep crisis right now. We do not know just what the future holds for us, but we know that the Lord has been preparing us for such a time as this so that we may be seeking His face that His Spirit can be free to restore the testimony of Jesus in this land."

Malawi

W HAT A DELIGHTFUL MEMORY! IT involves a letter we received from a man in Malawi. We had visited that African country many years before. It has a delightful national slogan, "The warm heart of Africa."

The letter was from a man who had been imprisoned for years, and would be in prison for years to come. A copy of a book I had written, which was published in America, had found its way into the prison library.

He had read it repeatedly, and wanted a copy for himself, which I gladly sent him of course. It was simply wonderful to read that this prisoner had had a change of heart and was determined to please God and help people for the rest of his life. I have never lost the joy of receiving letters like this one from 'darkest Africa'.

Perhaps I shall add that when we had visited Malawi those years before I had agreed to speak at a leaders retreat that was held at a camp-site that seemed to be far from any town. The same native food was served up continually. For me, with my kind of stomach, it was a challenge to eat it at all, let alone thankfully.

One day we were several times proudly told that the next day we would be served a European meal in our honour. At noon the next day the cook proudly marched in with it, smiling widely. What was the meal? Cold, greasy omelette! But it was served with beaming pride and generous love and we were grateful.

When we received an invitation to speak at that conference I had accepted it with a proviso limiting the number of times I would speak to twice a day. This was solely that I could 'be at my best' and share the word of the Lord with the maximum anointing possible. It was a shock to find that I had been scheduled to speak in six sessions each day. Twice a day is actually too much for me. I have no desire to be a robotic talking machine!

On the second day I told the missionary in charge of the retreat that I would stretch myself to speaking three times a day for the next few days, although I was not entirely comfortable with that. My suggestion was that if I spoke in the first, third and fifth session the other meetings could be taken up with discussion and response.

He still demanded that I speak six times each day, saying, "You are insulting these men. Some of the village pastors have walked many hours to get here." I replied that he was insulting both the Lord and me, and asked if he hadn't noticed how many of those men dozed off in the afternoon sessions.

At lunch time he told me that there was now general agreement that the afternoon sessions would be cancelled. In later sessions when I received questions from those gathered, there were probing questions that inferred strong criticism of the missionaries. When I met with some of the missionaries alone later I told them, "I let you guys off the hook today" but you know whether their critical questions are justified or not." There is plenty of variety in a travelling ministry!

Kenya

W E HAVE ONLY STOPPED OVER IN Kenya once. I flew there from Johannesburg ahead of Mary who followed me a day or two later. We stayed one further night in Nairobi and then flew on to London.

The purpose for my going there was to visit and encourage Chris Doust from the Cheam Fellowship in England. Who could but admire a young woman like this leaving behind family, friends and home comforts so that she could serve her Lord in a distant land. Chris had come down to Nairobi to meet me and we flew on a small missionary plane to the remote area where she worked.

The equator runs through the middle of Kenya and it certainly felt like it when we stepped out of that plane at the mission station. To me the heat seemed fierce night and day while I was there. The only noticeable indication of the airstrip was two lines of stones painted white running along each side of it. I didn't see a blade of grass anywhere.

There were only two missionary women living

and working at the station now, Chris and her fellow worker, a nurse I believe, who came from Ireland. That sister had a full set of tapes from a conference I had spoken at in Donegal, Ireland. She spoke of the blessing she had received through listening to them. Small world!

In the late afternoon Chris and I strolled out around the property chatting about Cheam and also the challenges she felt here in Kenya. At one point I joked that I would report her to the Cheam elders, but actually I appreciated her dedication and efforts more than ever. Had a pipeline broken? Chris fixed it. Did tyres need changing on the jeep, or wouldn't the vehicle start? Chris attended to things like that and much more besides.

As Chris and I strolled along a tribesman appeared over a sand dune with a spear in one hand, a bone stuck through his nostrils and only wearing a dirty loincloth. I inevitably lifted my camera to take his photo. Up came his spear and out flowed a torrent of words that were totally unintelligible to me. Chris quickly said, "Put the camera down now," which I did, and then she spoke mollifying words to the man involved. I had no idea that he would imagine I could take his soul captive in my camera by snapping his photograph.

I slept in an upstairs room in a separate building from the young women. Windows were open on both sides of my room to catch any breeze that might come that way. Actually, even the breeze was hot. I slept under a mosquito net without clothes, just lying on a sheet, and even that seemed unpleasantly hot. Several times through the night I got up and splashed myself with water to cool down a little.

The next morning I noticed a tap on another building that was releasing a solitary drip of water every four or five seconds. Under it a little bird squatted patiently with open mouth, catching each drip as it fell. After a while, when the bird flew off, another bird immediately took its place, so that not one drop of water was lost. I found myself thanking God for the water of life that He provides unstintingly to all who place their trust in Him.

On more than one occasion in that primitive area tribesmen have raided the place. Chris felt that she hadn't been brave enough when bullets started coming through her bedroom walls! I suspect that many another person wouldn't have made it to the bathroom that night, and would have headed for their homeland the next day!

When Chris had to drive some seriously injured, bloodied, and perhaps dying, tribes-person many miles over rough country to a clinic or hospital, a journey many hours long, she was a little ashamed of how her body reacted to the situation. Many an able bodied man wouldn't have been willing to undertake such a task at all. In my book, such a person needs to be highly honoured and respected.

Time spent in situations such as I saw on this visit, and had encountered in tribal areas in southern African countries, as well as in parts of India, brings a person to be exceedingly grateful for the comparative wealth of even the poorer people in the western world. We should be continually thankful to God because we are so very favoured and blessed.

A God-filled Nobody

Part 5

Europe

A God-filled Nobody

England

AFTER OUR FIRST VISIT TO AFRICA WE FLEW on up to England. For a month we moved around speaking in Anglican churches, Baptist churches, house church groups and, I think, an Elim church. Everyone was gracious and kind to us and yet I didn't really feel comfortable anywhere.

Towards the end of the month I commented to Mary, "If, twenty or thirty years from now I tell you that I am going back to England, please remind me how much I have hated being here now." My difficulty was my own and not with the land or the people. Somehow, I just didn't seem to fit in anywhere.

I felt uncomfortable with what seemed to be a mixture of apathy and self-satisfaction in the groups I visited. I saw the danger of believers being proud of their past without having any expectation of anything fresh and new from God today.

At one place where I was speaking at gatherings in a Church of England, I received a request from the elders of a nearby Strict Baptist church. In response, we visited them for an hour or two. I can still hear the pride in their voices as they showed me a plaque commemorating the martyrdom of one of their members several centuries before.

Why did they want to meet with me? They were about to call a new minister. The one who had recently left had stayed with them for years longer than they had wished. They had nothing good to say about the poor man. One of the things he had preached against strongly was the 'Charismatic Movement'. I understand that he had preached against other things they all felt were fully acceptable.

Now they had the opportunity to call a charismatic minister, and felt that must be a good idea since the other man had opposed it. They knew nothing of this movement and felt that, as a Baptist minister, I might be able to give them some balanced information. I gave them a full description of what to expect, feeling that if they were to proceed with calling the man, they would not be surprised by whatever he introduced. I did hope that such a man would minister with grace and wisdom.

This brings to mind a leaders' conference that I once attended in New Zealand, but didn't really enjoy. The announcement of the topic the next speaker had selected caused a fine Maori brother, Norman Tawhiao to ask me, "John, what is balance?" My reply was, "Norman, every man there will tell you that it was what they have!" We all think that it is the other person who lacks balance, don't we? I didn't bother attending that session.

In the last week before we flew on to the USA we spent a couple of days sharing in a house church group in Blackheath. At the start of our time there I had mentioned to Mary that we only had Wednesday evening free before leaving the country, and we should not commit ourselves to anything for that night.

On our first evening at Blackheath, Robert and Heather Stockwell came from the Cheam Fellowship. The next evening they brought several other folk. They stayed and chatted afterwards, and asked if we would visit their fellowship the next Sunday. Happily I told them that we were going to America on the Saturday. When they asked if we could come at all I said, "Only if it was suitable for Wednesday night." Mary immediately said, "No John," thus reminding me of our discussion. I explained to the folk what Mary and I had previously discussed.

I was also able to tell Mary that I now perceived that the evening had been reserved for this purpose. As it happened, our Thursday and Friday arrangements fell through, so I phoned the Stockwells to ask if we could come on the Wednesday and stay there until we flew out on the Saturday, to which they happily agreed. If we had not gone to Cheam I doubt if I would have ever returned to that part of the world again.

We had enjoyed our conversation with the Cheam leaders who had been able to come over to Blackheath, and immediately felt comfortable and 'at home' in the fellowship. Here were precious people who loved the Lord very deeply, and who expressed their devotion to Him in fragrant worship. There was delightful freedom from empty phrases and valueless repetitiveness, and an earnest desire to hear from the Lord. These pure-hearted believers obviously had open hearts to hear the 'now' word of the God.

Cheam made all the difference for us. We readily agreed to return at some time in the future, as the Holy Spirit might direct. This subsequently enabled us to have considerable input into the Cheam Fellowship, and elsewhere besides, including a visit to the Netherlands and several visits to Sweden.

During those first few days in Cheam, we were invited to meet Seymour and Marie Rice from Dublin, Ireland. I understand that their daughter Eleanor, who lived in Cheam at that time, had phoned over to them about us, saying something like, "This is a man for Ireland." I would not give an immediate answer to their invitation to visit Dublin, but assured them that I would pray about it. By then I had learned that I sometimes missed God's highest purposes if I responded too quickly to requests for ministry. After all, I did have a card on my desk, in the days of being a minister, that read, "If I think that I can do everything for everybody, then I think I am God."

When I gave that "I will pray about it" reply to a leader in Johannesburg at one time, he was obviously displeased with me. "All you preachers are the same," he told me, "When you don't have the courage to say no to our face you hide behind that 'I will pray about it' term." Maybe some do, I don't know. All I know is that I later accepted that particular invitation. A quality friendship soon built up between us.

Return Visits

W E HAVE VISITED THE CHEAM FOLK many times since then, at times briefly, and on other occasions for many months. Of particular blessing, as far as I am concerned, was the precious spiritual and friendly companionship we shared with the fellowship leaders. They were Michael and Jill Conrathe, Michael and Pam Campbell, Robert and Heather Stockwell, Bruce Dick and Eleanor whom he married in between some of our visits. Pam is in heaven now. I loved these elders at first meeting, and still do today.

Although Stan and Mavis Firth were not involved in the fellowship at that time, they have long since become good friends whom we esteem highly. These delightful people 'adorn the doctrine' with refreshing godliness.

Once, when we were in South Africa Robert and Heather Stockwell came and visited us. They brought a request that we spend six months with the Cheam folk, especially helping the elders walk in the fullness of God's purposes for them. After we agreed to go, I jokingly asked Robert for a job description!

He sent one to us that had been prepared by Pam Gathercole. Most of it was simple fun, and yet there was meaning in it too, as it was expressed in the terminology of erecting a building, starting with clearing the building site.

The only thing I remember on that job description was the injunction to rid the building site of all unwanted rubbish. My reply was that getting rid of that kind of junk wasn't difficult. It was any rubbish that they wanted to keep that would be a challenge. It always is!

Our proposed six months there actually lasted considerably longer. Here is how Mary described to folk in our retirement village why our departure from Cheam was delayed back then:

"On one occasion when we were in Cheam, Surrey, I suffered a sudden stroke. Initially I lost consciousness, was scarcely able to walk a few paces even with assistance, and often felt that cobwebs were cloaking my brain so that my speech was sheer gibberish.

"I knew that I had to walk. At first that simply meant getting out of my bed and walking around to the other side. John helped me with simple word games and patiently walking with me even though the first time he drove me to a park to walk he virtually had to carry me back to the car after about 70 or 80 paces. I knew that I had to persist with walking, and in retirement I still do,—as well as enjoying swimming exercises at the Christchurch QE2 aquatic centre two or three mornings a week."

One evening while Mary was almost bedridden she suddenly spoke to me, "I am thinking of going to heaven." I facetiously told her that I planned to do the same some time. Of course I quickly put an arm around her and asked if she was worried in any way. Her face was absolutely radiant as she replied, "Oh no, it is so wonderful."

At that time many of the Cheam folk went for a week's holiday convention at Kinmell Hall in Wales, and we went with them. It was a joy to share the word of the Lord there. In the evenings, the young folk especially, but all who wanted to, gathered in the large library area. I felt a bit like an old patriarch, sitting there, answering questions that the young people had previously written out, or which they asked there and then.

I recall one of the morning gatherings when an Irishman spoke out saying, "This dying is so painful!" It was dying to selfishness and wilful sin he was talking about. He had told me the same thing months before, so I said to him, "Michael, I hate slow, lingering deaths. Die now! Take up your cross now, and follow Christ."

How vitally important are Paul's words, "I have been crucified with Christ, and I no longer live, but Christ lives in me. The life I live in the body, I live by faith in the Son of God, who loved me and gave himself for me." Paul was writing about his daily 'walk' in the midst of an ungodly world.

Multitudes of believers are only half-alive spiritually, because they are neither really dead to self, nor truly walking the Calvary road. Little wonder that relative powerlessness and ineffectiveness are so wide-spread in the body of Christ. Little wonder too, that believers frequently lack the capacity to clearly and consistently hear the inner voice of the Holy Spirit—thus needing to rely on frequently garbled messages being passed on second-hand to them.

Mary was still ill while we were at Kinmell Hall, necessitating her having to spend most of the time in bed. Timmy Bateson came to visit us and enquire about Mary. At the time he was an elder in a house church somewhere in the London area. We first met him when he was acting in some kind of play that was showing in Johannesburg.

As we talked together he mentioned a fellow elder who was ill and unable to leave his bed. I asked him, "What percentage of him is ill?" Naturally, he replied, "John that is a stupid question. I have just told you he can scarcely lift his head off his pillow. Why do you ask that?"

I agreed that it seemed to be a stupid question, but, just maybe, it was the Lord. I had never thought in that kind of way before. So I said to Timmy, "Perhaps the question should be, how much of a man is physical? Is he spiritually ill? Is he emotionally or mentally ill?" After a moment's thought Timmy smiled and said, "Actually, when I think about it, only a small percentage of the man is ill!"

Over recent years when concerned friends have inquired about my health I have included in my reply that I am fully alive. Sometimes I even joke that most parts of me work quite well!

This may be the right place to mention that for many years now I have been able to tell folk that one of the best things the Holy Spirit ever did for me was to set me free to be me. What a great release! There is no need for my life to be cloned out of the expectations, beliefs and life-patterns of other believers. I refuse to accept pressure to 'toe the party line,' follow some group's predetermined doctrinal position, or fit into any man-made system or human ideal of the church.

Having stated that, let me add that I deeply appreciate and enjoy fellowship with brothers and sisters in Christ. If a person truly has faith in Christ, that is my brother or my sister, regardless of differences between us. I recall being asked at a service in the midst of an inter-church convention I was sharing at in New Zealand, "How can you accept Catholics?" My answer was, "I don't. I accept whoever the Lord accepts, refusing to be bothered with man-made labels."

I am very willing to hear the word of God through anyone, and hopefully receive with all humility whatever is truly of the Spirit. At the same time I refuse to deviate from a God-given path because of what someone may think of me, how they may rate me, or even if they reject me. It is enough for me to be aware that I am answerable to God Himself.

Reversion: An Ever Present Danger

AT ONE OF THE CHEAM LEADERS' gatherings I commented, "You men are in danger of reversion." When they asked me to speak on that at another meeting I agreed too quickly to do it. I had not thought in those terms before, and saw it as an interesting challenge. I had to sort myself out before the Lord over that hasty response. God is gracious!

Naturally I sought the Lord for understanding about reversion, and for clear revelation on how to speak of it. My desire was to be able to share a way forward without being critical or negative in any way. I have sometimes told leaders that we have a building function. Any idiot can tear a building down, but it takes a tradesman to erect one. Carping criticism and repeated negativism are tools of the devil.

During one night I was given insight on the matter. Reversion comes from walking in yesterday's revelation. I was to show a way to walk in what we are now hearing from the Lord, not in what has previously been heard—sometimes centuries earlier.

This is not to call for all the past to be ignored or carelessly discarded, but it is a call to be continually sensitive to what God says to us now. We need to hold lightly enough to what we have previously heard so that it never becomes a hindrance to walking in fresh revelation. Much of what God tells us is only for a season. Do we hear too quickly, for example, when we are instructed by the Lord to set up a committee and start something new? Yet far too slowly when He wants us to end it?

I saw that wherever the predictability factor is too high, the revelatory factor is too low. How often the Holy Spirit prompts us to speak or act in a certain way in church gatherings or elsewhere. When a similar situation arises we act as if we don't need to hear from God again, we will just do it the same as previously. How much we lose out on, when the Lord may have purposed something fresh and new for us.

Christendom is dotted with a multitude of groups who left one kind or other of church structure, to move into something simpler or freer or purer or different in some other way. Before many years have passed, the same kind of routine predictability, and the same sort of human control, returns, sometimes with renewed force even though in different trap-pings.

Before sharing these things with those men at that time, I earnestly sought grace from the Lord to be consistently true and real in my own life. I commit-ted myself afresh to be walking in what I am hearing from then on out. I have always liked the title of one of the books I wrote, but that is now out of print. It is: "Revelatory Adventure." As long as we live we should be able to maintain a spirit of adventure, shouldn't we?

Scotland

OUR FIRST VISIT TO SCOTLAND WAS in response to an invitation from Charlie and Chris Paterson, whom we had met in Pittsburgh Pennsylvania. I shall mention that in a passage covering our first visit to the USA. The Patersons met us in Aberdeen and drove us to their home in a fishing village named Cairnbulg. Their delightful home is built of really large stones fitted together to give exterior walls a couple of feet thick, which is more than enough to cope with both bitter cold and the fierce winds coming off the North Sea. Their friendly, caring hospitality was deeply appreciated.

I read of revival in the fishing villages up and down that coast, which took place in about 1920 until about 1922. In a two-week period about 900 residents of this village of 1,500 people, were converted. Out in fishing vessels, and in homes ashore, sin hardened and life hardened people were being convicted of their sin. In some cases they spontaneously cried to the Lord for salvation. Similar things were happening in other villages.

I am not sure whether the church Charlie and Chris

attended came into existence then, but it certainly sprang into life at that time. To be honest, there was no evidence of pulsating and sparkling spiritual life when we were there. While we were eating our mid-day meal an elder contacted the Patersons saying that the elders had met after the morning service. They had agreed that my ministry was orthodox, and they would allow me to speak in the evening service as well. I wasn't sure if that was complimentary or not! The minister was away at the time so had no part in this.

Over the years I have visited several places where there is a record of revival blessing somewhere in the past, and not always the very distant past. I have also chatted with men who have come from places where there had been recent reports of revival. There is no need to be pedantic about what 'revival' means, of course, because it has meant different things in different situations.

Revival is a resurgence of spiritual life resulting in the transformation of lives so that God is won-derfully glorified. It brings believers into a much deeper awareness of Christ's presence with them, introduces them to early church lifestyles and radically affects their daily lives. Almost invariably the dramatic change of believers' lives, as well as the direct sovereign work of the Holy Spirit, results in unbelievers turning to the Lord.

I have read that during the Welsh Revival someone from England visited a town or village where revival had been reported. He approached the local policeman and asked, "Excuse me, but can you tell me where the revival is?" The reply was classic, "Certainly sir," said the copper. He pointed to the front of his tunic, saying, "Right under this button."

Is revival a sovereign act of divine grace, or is it God's response to earnest intercession? I suspect both. We know, for example, something of the revival that swept England under John Wesley, George Whitfield and others. Yes, it was a sovereign work of God, but you cannot discount the value of the 'holy club' of radical young believers that Wesley was involved with. Whether you think of the moving of God in the Hebrides, the Congo, the mid-century revivals in America, or other such wonderful occasions, you will discover a deep persistent heart cry in at least a few of God's people.

An elder of a church I pastored was not totally

happy with my ministry. His wife told him that 'our' local church was close to revival, and to take care what he did to that man—me. He told us this at an elders' meeting, but demanded that I conform to what he felt was seemly for a minister. "After all," he said, "there have been many revivals in history where people haven't raised their hands." He also stated that it wasn't revival preaching to condemn avarice and crooked business practice, as I had on occasion. Perhaps it was 'too close to the bone.'

I declared that the price to that church for revival in the city, was the laying down of our lives and the death of that church. Such language was not unanimously acceptable!

There is no doubt in my mind that in such special times the Holy Spirit requires somewhat unusual things of those who are totally yielded to Him. Of themselves they are valueless and should not become the focus of attention or response. As a test of our commitment, they may be crucial as proof of our personal cross bearing.

I am thinking of a question that I was once asked, "John, where will the stigma be next?" There has always been stigma attached to radical Christian living, since such a life-style makes plain that we are not of this world, even as Christ was not of this world. We are creatures of eternity.

Now the tragedy is that long after the fire has gone out, or at least died way down, people will often place value on some kind of external factor, while losing sight of what is vital, internal and eternal. When everything is boiled down, as we say, the heart of the matter is the matter of the heart. That fact needs underlining in all of our memories.

Perhaps there is wisdom in the thought that man cannot initiate, engineer or bring revival. It is an activity of God, by divine grace. However, it is possible for man to delay, hinder or quell revival blessings.

A year or two later those Cairnbulg elders dismissed their pastor because he adopted an external stance which was incompatible with what God had done back in the 1920s. That is tragic, not for the pastor, but for themselves and the witness of Christ in the area. When we returned to stay with Charlie and Chris several years later we were delighted to share the word of the Lord in homes, and also in well-attended meetings in a hired hall.

Once when we were in Cheam John Larkum introduced us to Jim and Anne Bell. At the time Jim was minister of the Congregational Church in Cumbernauld, Scotland. At the same time he was hungry for reality in every aspect of his life. It was a pleasure for Mary and me to stay with them after our visit to Cairnbulg. We were with them for about a week I think, during which time I preached in that church and also shared in quite a number of various fellowship groups around the area.

Not too long after that Jim resigned from the church and took up school teaching while being active in informal church situations. Jim and Anne visited us on our return trip to Cairnbulg and again we went to stay with them for a day or two. Their pure hearts, earnestness, spiritual freshness and sincere desires for God's glory blessed us anew. Jim commented to me that although we had never spent much time with them, yet our visits had always been during cross-road situations, and very beneficial to them.

Sweden

WE HAVE VISITED SWEDEN ON SEVERAL occasions, meeting delightful people and speaking in various gatherings. Robert and Heather Stockwell accompanied us on one of these visits, and on another David and Nina Rice and one or two others from Dublin were with us for some days in a lovely Christian camp.

In Stockholm, Lennart and Berit Rausch provided caring hospitality on more than one occasion. I well remember a leaders' day of meetings in Cheam that Lennart attended. I always felt such gatherings were a privilege and delight. Lennart had recently undergone a course of chemotherapy, and was not to live much longer, but that day he was simply radiant with the deep inner peace and joy that only God can give. What a blessing!

We have enjoyed meeting Leif and Britt Strömberg on a number of occasions, both in Sweden and when they visited Ireland. One of the unique privileges in our kind of life style has been to meet brothers and sisters in various parts of the world, and immediately feel a close love tie with them in the Spirit. Obviously, it is all a part of Jesus saying, "I will build my church," an extension of which must surely be, "It will be My way, or no way!"

Without recalling the situation, I remember a time when I was the only 'foreigner' staying with the Rausch family. Their daughter Elizabeth, who is a fine young woman now and married to Andrew Langran, the son of our dear Dublin friends Colin and Joyce, was a little child then. Berit told me she was asking if I could speak Swedish. My answer, "No." She persisted, asking, "Can't he speak one word of Swedish." I couldn't, and Berit passed it on.

"Please tell her that I can love in Swedish," I requested. As Berit did that I held out my arms and she joyfully responded. After that she would take me for walks in their garden, holding my hand and chatting away cheerily in Swedish. I talked to her in English. Neither of us seemed to care about the language barrier. More than once when we were having a meal I may have been overlooked for a minute or two, but Elizabeth would speak out. All I heard of it was "... Papa, John, Papa, John ..." Immediately adults would look in my direction, and take care that I lacked nothing.

A God-filled Nobody

Berit interpreted with great skill for me whenever I spoke in meetings. I recall commenting once, as an aside really, that those gathered should take care not to rely too heavily on speakers from other countries to the extent that local men were ignored.

While we were all sitting down at the end of my sharing, Sam Ekholm, [who has recently passed away] came forward and put his hands around my neck quite firmly. An interesting moment! Then he told me, "Foreigners have had us like that for years." He pronounced the 'g' of foreigners the same as in the word messengers. Sam told me that evening that he was involved with the European Atomic Energy Commission. He said that there were sufficient atomic weapons in the world at that time to destroy everyone on the face of the earth, sixteen times over! Isn't it precious to rest in the fact that our times are in God's hands?

Ireland

PRIOR TO ONE OF OUR TRIPS OVERSEAS, we, with three other couples who were close friends, drove out of Hamilton towards Cambridge, New Zealand, and spent the weekend together in a motel that overlooks the Waikato river. Apart from enjoying friendly fellowship with Gordon and Margaret Pellow, Brian and Alison White and Warren and Anna Young, we were spending time waiting on the Lord. We all desired Father's rich blessing to be on the coming ministry journey, and were seeking to be particularly sensitive to anything the Holy Spirit may wish to impress on us.

One afternoon as we were on our knees before the Lord, Brian spoke to me. "I am seeing a picture," he said. "In Ireland there is a large stone or cement walled house with a painted green door, a high wrought-iron style of front fence and a long path up to the house." With real conviction he added that my future ministry in Ireland would involve relationship with those people.

Following that, we undertook our first visit to the Emerald Isle, which quickly became special and precious to us because of the warm-hearted people that we soon came to know there. We were met at the airport by the kind of man one warms to immediately. When he drove to his home, there was a house exactly as Brian White had described.

When we went to our bedroom Mary asked me, "Did you recognise this house?" "How on earth could I?" I replied, "We have never been here before." She reminded me of Brian's vision. I hadn't thought any more about it, and was happy to just leave it with the Lord. All I wanted to do was honour Him and be a blessing to His people.

One time in Pennsylvania a man asked me how to raise his son to be a prophet. When I enquired about this strange question, he told me that a preacher who had visited their fellowship had prophesied that one his boys would become a prophet. I cannot recall what had been 'prophesied' about the other son. I am convinced that there is much, much less pure prophetic expression in the church on earth today, than many people believe.

I advised that man, as I have advised others elsewhere who have asked a similar sort of question, to forget the prophecy regardless of whether it was genuinely a message from God or not. "Teach your son by example and instruction," I counselled, "To love the Lord with all his heart, and to set a course in life in which he wholeheartedly responds to whatever God asks of him." The last thing the church needs is another assembly-line clone-like product of human engineering!

The day after we arrived in Dublin Seymour and Marie Rice drove us up to Donegal. The route took us across into Northern Ireland, and then across back into the Republic again. We thoroughly enjoyed the conference in which Catholics, Protestants, and many other believers who made no claim to be in either of those groups, mingled happily together. It was a pleasant privilege to be one of the two speakers.

After one gathering I chatted with a Catholic nun. Foolishly, I asked where she was from, and then when she told me I had to admit that I didn't know where the place was. In response to her surprised, "You don't know where it is?" I asked her forgiveness, mentioning that I had only been in Ireland a few days. Wasn't it lovely that she had not thought of me as a foreigner at all?

A God-filled Nobody

As Seymour drove us back to Dublin, a considerable journey, we enjoyed times of chatting together, and times of simply watching the countryside about us. At one point as we drove along a road that had trees by the roadside a man jumped out onto the road and waved out for us to stop. Rather than that, Seymour instantly accelerated.

After we were well past the area I asked Seymour why his instinctive response had been to speed up, whereas many of us would have started to slow down. I was soon enlightened. Why was the man there without a vehicle when there was nobody else around, as far as we could see? Why did he want us to stop? In those days drivers who stopped in a situation like that could at least have had their car taken from them to be used as a booby trap with dynamite hidden in it. The driver and their passengers could have literally been in mortal danger as well.

Love Ties in the Spirit

F OR US, THOSE DAYS IN DONEGAL WERE the beginning of a deep-calls-unto-deep kind of closeness with many of the folk who had come up from Dublin and other places as well. Some who come to mind are David and Nina Rice, Lionel and Susan Hogan, John and Rose Ennis [Rose is in heaven now], Alan and Yvonne Walsh, Colm and Cloida Morris, David and Joy Ebbs and Tom and Barbara McDonagh. We later came to know well and love deeply Colin and Joyce Langran, Con and Olive Ryan and Tommy and Anneli Hayes.

Then there are their families and others who were young adults at that time. We have also observed the growth of those who were children then. To me it has been quite moving to have these who are young adults now, invite me, an old man now, to spend an evening with them sharing the word of the Lord.

There is no group on earth that we love more dearly, nor with whom we feel such a oneness as these I mention and many more there beside.

Mary, as others in New Zealand, has sometimes

commented on my whole-hearted devotion to the Lord as a young man. My one desire, far above everything else, was to see Him as glorified as He should be so that He found deep satisfaction in His people, and so that there could be an enormous in-gathering of souls. Now and again over the years I have asked God if there couldn't be at least one generation in history where a large majority of unbelievers in this wicked world would come to the cross. Could it not be this generation?

I have written that last paragraph so that I can emphasise the deep joy we have through coming to know brothers and sisters of a like heart there in Ireland. We share a close oneness with these precious friends. I feel so comfortably one with fellow believers who set their hearts to walk in clear and consistent spiritual hearing.

There are many ways in which Christians become joined with others, but the only linkage I feel totally comfortable with in the body of Christ is a love bond in the Spirit. Other joining seems to inevitably involve human control which so easily results in bondage and perpetual immaturity.

We have seen changes in lives and changes in the

way these Irish friends do things. Whenever some of them come together, they know the reason for that specific meeting, [using 'meeting' in the broadest sense]. We have noted a loving, caring, supporting, accepting and encouraging attitude being lived out in daily lives.

Here are people who understand that there is a season for everything under the sun. A season has a beginning and an ending. Too often, I believe, church folk are possibly far too quick to start something, and definitely far too slow to even consider bringing it to an end. That path leads to bondage and endless activity that can be largely futile.

John Ennis brought a friend to see us when we on one of our visits to Dublin. As part of our conversation, the friend mentioned that I, with others, don't have open-air meetings, which he felt was most remiss. My reply? "Of course we do, every time the Lord directs us to." He asked about prayer meetings, Gospel meetings, and I don't remember what else. My answer was always the same.

I have set my heart to respond to the Holy Spirit in whatever he asks of me. The fact that it's half a lifetime since I have received any indication whatever from the Lord to be involved in an 'open-air meeting' is of no consequence. He is Lord of my life, not tradition, custom, or human expectation.

On some of our visits to Ireland Mary and I were provided a home for ourselves, which is quite important on longer stays, and deeply appreciated. On our last visit together, John Ennis had freely and lovingly handed us his home, spending those weeks with a son and daughter-in-law. He had gone to great lengths to prepare the place for our coming.

We frequently had 'open home' for breakfast, with anything from one or two to half a dozen or more joining in. What choice fellowship we enjoyed! There was a delightful blend of friendly camaraderie and of sharing at a spiritual level. We were very aware of the Lord's presence, and so in a sense, without any ritual, we were really breaking bread together.

There are two things I recall sharing at those breakfasts. John was telling us about the honey on the table, where it came from, and why it was the best in the land—or was it the best in the world? After some time I asked those present that morning,

"Have you had any honey from the Rock lately?" There was no lack of sharing at that point.

It must have been at our last such breakfast that I mentioned that during the night I had been asking Father if there was anything else He wanted to give me to share with these good friends. I believe His answer was for me to tell them that I have passed on the baton, so I did.

Such a statement could be interpreted variously, of course. That is why I have often told folk that if they receive some kind of revelation from the Lord they will need further revelation to understand it, rather than depending on natural reason for interpretation. God can give an unmistakable inner 'knowing'.

Fellow 'Kiwis' Allan and Ruth Bell brought Ed and Sheila to visit us in New Zealand. Allan asked about my health. I asked them all a question, "Would you prefer to talk about my health, or to talk about Jesus." Everyone chose the latter. The fact that, unknown to them, I had only come out of hospital a few days before was of no lasting consequence.

Sometimes Christians seem to feel a bit awkward

in informal, everyday situations about discussing spiritual things with another believer. One thing we encouraged in those Dublin breakfasts is for everyone to be alert for the right question to ask. One evening, eight or ten couples met at Con and Olive Ryan's for a meal. It would also give me an opportunity to share the word of the Lord with them.

Have you ever noticed at such gatherings that a whole meal can go enjoyably by without any discussion or comment at a spiritual level? All the conversation is about work, family, sport, or other such things, none of which are wrong in themselves, of course. After the meal, we change gears and get into a different mode in which we open up to the areas that are really more vital and of more interest to us than all the rest.

There is always a danger, I suppose, of having 'water tight' compartments in our lives where spiritual thought and activity fit in. Wouldn't God's purpose be for a delightful blend of natural and spiritual, social and devotional aspects of life?

That night at Ryan's I simply asked a few questions during the meal, requesting one word answers. The first was asking those fine young women what was the most necessary ingredient in being a godly wife. After discussion and further eating I asked the men a similar question. A combination like that makes for wonderful dining!

Here and There

I CLEARLY REMEMBER A WELL ATTENDED meeting that was called to celebrate the coronation of Jesus as King of all Ireland. We dressed for the occasion, with lovely dresses, suits, and button-holes all adding to the atmosphere. We had in mind the account of David being anointed King by Samuel long before Israel recognised him as such. In very truth he was king, even though not widely acknowledged at the start. Those who allowed him to be their king shared the benefits of his reign. With joyful praise and tender worship we lauded the King of kings and Lord of lords, to whom be glory for ever and ever.

In conjunction with one of our visits it had been arranged to hold a week's family holiday at Portrush up in the North. An unforgettable part of this was that we all came together only a few times, and yet there was a delightful freedom and fullness in the informal chatting around the tables at meal times, in twos and threes that sat here or there, or went on walks and outings together. To be among people who maintain a vibrantly alive love relation with our dear Lord Jesus virtually guarantees fragrant times of sharing our lives and His together. A beautiful blend!

There were folk who came over from England, up from South Africa, and down from Sweden for that week, and for the following one in Dublin. Allan and Ruth Bell from New Zealand were also there. Well before we arrived in the country the Dublin folk decided before the Lord that they wouldn't set a charge or fee for attendance. Those who wanted to voluntarily gave whatever they felt was right towards the considerable costs involved. Because of their generosity, every cost was met beforehand.

At the end of the week we travelled down to Dublin, with the overseas visitors being the guests of local families. This provided for a lovely blend of family life in conjunction with some joint pleasure activities during the day, and on some evenings a public meeting which was held in the Wesley College assembly hall.

Different men spoke in those gatherings, including myself. The purpose agreed on ahead of time was to make available to the wider church whatever we were hearing from the Lord during that fortnight. All along it had been our determination not to be involved to gain anything for ourselves—not pleasure, nor experience, nor blessing—but for this to be a season of bringing joyful pleasure to the Lord Himself. Of course it is impossible to out-give God, and many were deeply touched by the Lord, mightily encouraged and given further direction for the path ahead.

One of the things I love among our Irish friends is that they don't have a 'them' and 'us' mentality. Boundary lines dividing believers from believers are out of place. Altogether those weeks were superb.

From our first meeting with them, David and Nina Rice have held a special place in our hearts. We have stayed in their home a number of times, and have seen Joy and Anna grow from little children with their first skates, to fine, godly young women. Here is part of a letter Nina recently wrote to us:

"I find myself thinking of you very often these days, and just thought it would be good to say hello. So very much of what you have said seems to apply itself to our lives and we continually thank the Lord that He led us to find each other. Every day I'm appreciating more the song about the way of humility, and it does have to be daily ... the flesh always wants to go the other way.

"We are so enjoying our life here [in our new home]. I sometimes wonder if it can be right to be so happy on earth! This is such a beautiful place, though it has suffered from neglect and needs a lot of work to restore it. To walk with God in a garden, and to be able to do it every day, is an exquisite joy to me, and I feel so privileged. The best thing is to be able to entertain much more than we did before, and it's just lovely to let the Lord arrange our schedule and see people relaxed and blessed. This does not come naturally to me but truly His burden is light.

"Sometimes I long to be able to sit with you and talk about all sorts of things, visible and invisible. So much that is going on is quite perplexing, but I am reminded of a comment you made about only needing to be concerned with that which is of the light . . . simple, but a great safeguard.

"Well, really just wanted you to be assured that the love, the sacrifices, the faith you both invested in us is indeed bearing the fruit of thanksgiving to the dear Father of us all. Please pray for us that we do not miss any of the signposts on this new part of the road.

"Much, much love to both of you from David and me. Nina."

David is a high school teacher. I am glad that years ago he decided not to enter 'full time' ministry. I recall a businessman in Johannesburg coming to me after a Full Gospel Businessmen's luncheon and saying, "Guess what, brother Beaumont. The Lord has called me to be a fisher of men. I have just sold my business and am launching out."

To his amazement I commented to that fine, earnest man, "That is one of the strangest things I have heard." When he asked why, I replied that in the same breath he had told me he was becoming a fisherman, and then that he had just sunk his boat. Surely our boat is whatever takes us to where the fish are.

Now and again somebody has told me that the Lord has called him into full time work. I have to say frankly that I don't understand what they are talking about. It seems plain to me that God calls us to various functions and ministries [that is, servant roles]. If at times that makes secular employment impossible, then Father will supply our needs in a different way.

This is well typified in the life of the Apostle Paul. I can testify that the seasons of my life when I was temporarily involved in an 'ordinary' secular job were of as much value to me, and to the Lord, as other times when fully engaged in ministry, I believe. It is very carnal to look on 'full time ministry' as the 'officer' rank or class in the Lord's army!

Even though I have not written about it, Mary and I have been in other towns and cities in Ireland to share the love and joy of Jesus. Portadown and Coleraine in the North, and Ferns, Cork, and Mullingar in the Republic, are places that come to mind.

Several years ago I sent a message to Dublin friends from New Zealand, which simply said on the Lord's behalf, "Keep your eyes on Me, and drink from the river."

I had long believed that in the Bible, rivers typify a constant flow and a great abundance. At this time I realized that it also means living beside the river, and drinking from the source. How could Spirit filled believers be totally contented with being dished out a cupful of water now and again [i.e. Sunday mornings] that somebody else has brought from the river?

One Other Thing

ONCE WHEN I SHARED WITH A GROUP of believers in Kloof, Natal, South Africa, someone asked me to talk about our [then] recent visit to Ireland, which I did. Afterwards a man we knew quite well, who had a Catholic connection, told us that he had recently been to Ireland, sharing the gospel quite widely. Several times he exclaimed, "I never saw anything remotely like what you have spoken about!" He did not doubt my word, but was a little disappointed that he had missed something precious.

None of us see more than the minutest fraction of what God is doing anywhere on earth. Most of His activity is in human hearts. Besides that, only God can open the eyes of the blind. There have been times when I have earnestly asked Him to save me from selective blindness of any kind, and to open my eyes to all that He would have me see. There is always more!

Part 6

United
States
of
America

A God-filled Nobody

W E HAVE MET MANY WONDERFUL people on our quite numerous visits to the USA and have deeply appreciated the warm-hearted way in which we have been accepted. Brothers and sisters in cities and towns across twenty or more States have opened their hearts and homes to us, not a few becoming dear friends.

We are grateful for the multitude of opportunities given to us to share the life and love of Jesus in a wide range of situations and localities. It is a pleasure to share some of our experiences over the years. Our visits to that great country usually lasted from three to six months

From time to time we have been asked, "You travel a lot, so what do you see God doing?" No doubt this is a well-intentioned question, but we are very deeply aware that most of what God does is a hidden work in the hearts of individual people. None of us see more than the smallest fraction of it.

The above statements are made simply to mention that in a writing like this there inevitably has to be mention of the little snippets God has allowed us to see of the Holy Spirit's work. However it is well worth being reminded that although we have seen public response in many of the gatherings we have addressed over the years, no one can know how many have quietly responded to some word from the Lord. We have no need to know what the Lord has accomplished in such cases, either at the time or in subsequent years.

The last time I was in Zimbabwe someone mentioned several folk whose lives were touched and transformed by the saving grace of God when I had first spoken there many years previously. I did not need to know, but must say that it was encouraging to hear of it years later. Some of those dear ones are good friends today. Let us never become 'slaves to the visible.'

Our First Visit

ALTHOUGH I WILL NOT ATTEMPT TO PUT everything in chronological order, there are several things about our first visit that are worth commenting on. We flew into New York's JFK airport from England on a Saturday night and spoke in several services the next day. A day or so later we flew upstate to enjoy a few days at the well known Elim Bible College. Not only had friends of ours in New Zealand attended that College, but in my mind there was a link somehow with Jonathan Edwards whose story I had read and marvelled at.

To me he was a man with a burning heart for God. How could a short-sighted preacher read a sermon, "Sinners in the hands of an angry God," to his congregation and have them gripping their seats in God-wrought fear? His earnest, self-sacrificial praying for a spiritual outpouring had stirred my heart in the past as I had read about the 'mid-century revivals.' It is interesting to note that the sermon mentioned above is readily available from a number of web sites today. There is obviously a lot of interest in it almost two hundred and fifty years after Jonathan Edwards went to heaven.

We were warmly welcomed and I was given the opportunity to address the large student body at a chapel service. Our month long itinerary was supposed to have been arranged by a friend in N.Z. but not much had happened. A NZer there, with the College President's help, arranged for us to go to Pittsburgh and also to a place in Florida.

In Pittsburgh we had been told that we would be met by Mr. and Mrs. Smith. After our arrival at the airport we waited and waited, but no one came. We asked for these people to be paged, which was done, although we were told that it was like looking for a needle in a haystack in that large, teeming airport. Eventually Buzz and Doris Smith approached us. They were not there to meet us at all, but to meet a lovely couple from Scotland, Charlie and Chris Patterson. The Smiths were surprised that we were there. There had been a misunderstanding so that they were not expecting us at all!

With generous hearts they took us home anyway, and we had lovely fellowship with them and with the Pattersons from Scotland who were there, it seems, on a once-in-a-lifetime visit. On several later occasions we visited them in Scotland, enjoying lovely friendship as well as sharing the word of the Lord up in a fishing village named Cairnbulg, Grampian. I spoke in several services in Pittsburgh at that time, and returned on later visits to the USA.

Another Bible College

ON THAT FIRST VISIT WE ALSO WENT to a very different kind of Bible College, flying in to Charlotte, North Carolina, and being taken for what seemed to us to be a very long drive to Walhalla in South Carolina. We rode with the driver, named Wayne, in the front of a very dusty utility vehicle over unsealed roads, to a very modest school. I was a little surprised to learn that he was actually the Principal of the Faith Training Centre.

Our contact there had been through a man who had spent some time in New Zealand. Everyone knew him as brother Worley. He had founded this Bible school, and came and went, depending on whatever preaching arrangements he may have had elsewhere. We knew before we arrived that he was held in high esteem by many believers in many places. Some New Zealanders will never forget his visits to our country.

Brother Worley, and everyone else were very warm in their welcome. We loved it there. At one stage, when I was sharing the word of the Lord with the students, Brother Worley slipped out of the gathering. He had gone to tell a young woman working in the kitchen that she must come quickly because I was speaking exactly what was intended for her. She later confirmed that it had been. When Brother Worley spoke in a meeting he was very 'folksy,' every now and again chatting with someone sitting in the congregation. But the anointing of God was obviously on his life and ministry.

While we were in Walhalla there was a gathering of church leaders in which we participated. I was part of a panel invited to answer questions from students and visitors. Another person there was DeVerne Fromke from Indiana whom I had not met before, even though he had visited New Zealand. As a result of sharing time with those leaders we were invited to several other places to share the word of the Lord.

Quite Unusual!

I BELIEVE IT WAS OUR FIRST VISIT TO A PLACE not far from Saratoga in upstate New York. I had been invited to speak in a number of services. As I came to the end of a message I was sharing in one of these gatherings I paused in silence, looking to the Holy Spirit for instructions. I felt I knew what the pastor would do if I simply sat down, and I didn't feel that was what Father wanted. Responding to an inner persuasion of the Spirit I simply stood in silence. The pastor half stood to his feet but sat back again when he saw that I was not moving away or sitting down.

A man stood up near the back and slowly made his way to the front, getting down on his knees and then on his face before the Lord. Soon everyone seemed to be on their knees or on their faces, either at the front or among the seats. It all seemed to happen in slow motion, with a continuing hush seeming to have settled upon the place. A delightfully fragrant time ensued with a precious awareness of the Lord's presence among us in grace and power. As would be expected, after some considerable time sweet expressions of loving worship and thanksgiving swelled up from grateful hearts. It was as though a gentle breath of heaven had swept across every heart.

Wise Advice

ONE SUNDAY NIGHT I SPOKE IN THE Assembly of God in Bowie, Maryland. We had not been there before, but returned on several occasions in the future. It was one of those services where I felt especially 'free' and wonderfully anointed as I shared the word of the Lord. When I finished speaking, the pastor, who had left the platform to sit beside his wife as I spoke, stood to his feet and made his way forward. When he came to the stepped front of the platform he quietly sank to his knees quietly weeping and praying. Without anything being said, many others came forward also.

After moving among those who were praying for some time, I slipped down to the back of the sanctuary. There was a beautiful black brother there who hugged me. I had just noted the time and commented that I felt ashamed for having spoken at such length. The time must have just flown by, and it was late.

That dear brother said something to me that I have thought of from time to time over the years. It was, "Don't you out-God God." In other words, I heard him saying that in my natural mind I may be thinking I had spoken too long, but if it had all been under God's control and direction, as I was confident it had been, then I should not allow natural reason to intrude.

Watch the time

WE MINISTERED A NUMBER OF TIMES in an assembly in Virginia. On my first visit there I was taken by a delightful brother I was staying with, Warren Weaver, the Richmond head of Full Gospel Businessmen's Fellowship.

When we arrived at the church, Warren introduced me to the pastor who took us to his study. After a word or two of greeting, he told me two things. The first was that he wanted the service to conclude at 8 o'clock. I am not sure of his exact words, but he also said that he didn't want to have to spend time over the next month or two tidying up a mess caused by a visiting speaker. No doubt he had had some bad experiences with such preachers.

I was confident that no offense was intended, and I took none. However I did say, "Brother why don't you and I agree that you are not ready for my ministry. I will gladly sit in the congregation and bless you as you speak." I would have been content with that. However, Warren immediately said, "No, John." He and the pastor both told me to go ahead and speak and I somewhat hesitatingly agreed to do so.

To me the service seemed to be fine right from the start. I thought that the pastor had a good spirit and obviously loved his people. When introduced I proceeded to share the things God had laid on my heart for that hour. In finishing I said something like, "I am going to say something just once to you, and this is it: If you have definite and specific spiritual need and want the Lord to meet that need now, please stand to your feet."

At that, for the first time since I had started speaking I looked at my watch. It was exactly 8 o'clock so I turned to the pastor and quietly said, "Your meeting, brother." He told me to carry on, but I declined, pointing out that it was 8 o'clock. The dear man told me that he was only standing because he had definite and specific need! That being said I happily responded to his request. We were invited back on a number of occasions after that.

The Finger of God

BEFORE WE LEFT NEW ZEALAND ON one of our journeys our friends Gordon and Margaret Pellow, Brian and Alison White and Warren and Anna Young, joined Mary and me for a weekend away where we could wait on the Lord together. On one of the evenings as we were praying Brian asked me, "John, do you know what the finger of God is?" I told him that I didn't, meaning not in a sense applicable to that moment. He lightly touched my finger and said, the Holy Spirit says that this is the finger of God to you as you visit the various countries on your schedule.

If I remember aright, we were going to the USA first and then to England and Ireland before going down to South Africa and perhaps Zimbabwe. The trip would take at least a year. It was an interesting word that I accepted but set aside for specific quickening by the Holy Spirit whenever He selected the appropriate time or times. I had no desire to naturally interpret what the brother had passed on to me, or to take control of it and fit it into any preconceived ideas of my own.

In several situations in Pittsburgh, Pennsylvania,

this had special meaning. After a God-blessed service on a Sunday night our hosts took us out for coffee and pizza with some of their friends, one of whom had not been in the service. He was told about the events of the evening as many folk had responded publicly to the Lord's tug at their hearts.

That person was involved with a local Christian TV station. An outcome of this was an invitation for me to be interviewed on the channel, the next evening, I think. I was very tired and could only remember that I hadn't particularly enjoyed being interviewed on a TV station in the South. Accordingly, I did not agree to it until the next morning.

The interview started off with the usual kind of questioning until a person behind the cameras held up a board saying, "Ask him about the finger of God." The interviewer said to me, "My producer has told me to ask you about the finger of God. I don't know what that means, but tell me about the finger of God."

I spoke of the mature and godly brother in New Zealand who had first spoken to me about it, and then mentioned some interesting incidents, probably mostly from the previous evening—I don't remember. Following that I said, "Even as we sit here now, in my heart I can see some of the people viewing this [live] programme, but of course I cannot point to them.

"Yes you can," several voices spoke at once, with my interviewer adding, "Point over there." He was indicating one of the cameras. So I shared what I saw. I remember that I saw a woman with two sons, she had no idea where one of them was and ached to see him again. She knew where the other one was, and almost wished she didn't, because of the unsavoury situation he was in.

Among the others I spoke to there is only one I remember. "I see a boy who is ten or eleven years old," I said. I told him he was sitting there thinking tearfully that I was only pointing and speaking to adults. "Your loving heavenly Father knows the cry of your heart," I said. "You have lost your daddy and your mother is heart-broken, but the Lord Jesus knows and cares." Naturally I expanded what was said to each one.

The air seemed electric! A hum of whispered prayer came from production staff, cameramen and others. There was a line of telephonists sitting at the back of the studio. They were all rapidly engaged as calls started coming back in. In between my sharing with another person I could 'see' in my spirit, notes were handed to my interviewer who would read out that one person mentioned after another was calling in, sharing their joy and requesting prayer.

I have always been very conscious that such gifts are not given to embarrass and hurt anyone, but to demonstrate God's wonderful mercy and love and thus draw them to Him in a new and fresh way. As an aside I remember a pastor in New Zealand asking my co-pastor and myself, "What gifts do you guys minister with?"

My reply wasn't what was expected, and not fully accepted either! I said that I trusted Father for whatever gifts were necessary for effective ministry at any particular point of time. For example, what good would it be if a dear believer came to me needing revelation in a difficult situation when all I could say was, "I am sorry, but I only minister with a gift of healing."

I don't believe I have ever been given gifts of the Spirit to carry around with me. Rather, I have frequently been able to reach out and receive a gift from the Lord to pass on to the intended recipient. It was from Him for them. I was only passing it on, so how could I say that it was mine?

A Good Outcome

N FLORIDA, I WAS SPEAKING IN A SERIES of meetings at some church or other—an independent kind of place I think. The pastor and a few others took us to Denny's for a snack after an evening meeting. We had enjoyed the day and their conversation was enjoyable and interspersed with a bit of humour now and again.

From across the restaurant a man who had been sitting alone stood up and slowly walked over asking, "Are you from a club or church or something?" One of the guys answered him and invited him to sit with us. It turned out that he was a fisherman who had missed his boat and was hitch hiking to catch up with it at another port. He wasn't dressed well, and had no money, so the guys provided a meal for him.

And then, I could not believe my ears! One of the men asked Bill a religious question that was a bit like asking a toddler whether he had ever swum the Atlantic. It had no relevance and seemed to be the last question the poor guy should be asked. His reply was hilarious! He said, "Well, I used to go to a Baptist Sunday-School when I was young." We all roared with laughter. One of them pointed at me saying, "You should talk with him. He has been a Baptist minister."

Well, some time later we all went our happy ways, some of the men still laughing and asking each other that weird question. The next day I learnt that the man who had asked the question had provided the fisherman with motel accommodation and meals— probably some clothing as well.

All I know is that the next evening among the seekers that crowded the altar of prayer, was Bill with that initial questioner beside him. Bill's life was touched as he experienced salvation in Christ. He was given a Greyhound ticket to the port he was headed for. Don't you love the unpredictability that adds a sparkle to the ways of the Lord?

Canadian Geese

WE DROVE FROM MARYLAND DOWN through Virginia, and, after some meetings there, on to Tennessee, eventually to drive via Kentucky to Indiana. Our purpose in going to Tennessee was simply to spend a few days with an air-force officer and his wife who had moved from Maryland to a base there. We had an enjoyable time together and as a side issue we were given an interesting story about the nature of Canadian geese.

The base had a man-made lake on it, to which Canadian geese had made their way and settled in. Apparently the Base Commander had wanted the geese to be a permanent feature and so ordered that their wings should be clipped so that these migratory birds could not fly away at the change of season. It worked well and the geese stayed there for years.

Here is the punch line: Those birds became so accustomed to being restricted to that base that they no longer needed their wings clipped, and neither did their offspring. Now, we believers are intended to soar. We are meant to be seated with Jesus in the heavenly realms. We are equipped to be more than conquerors through Christ who loves us. God's purpose is that we be changed from one degree of glory to another. Peace like a river and joy unspeakable and full of glory are not simply whimsical ideals for a few idyllic high points in our lives. We are wonderfully favoured, blessed and fully provided for by our glorious heavenly Father of love.

What goes wrong? Do circumstances clip our wings, or does discouragement? Perhaps the bondage of man-made church dogma and practice dims our vision, drains away our freshness and locks us into mediocrity. There can be a new day for every one of us.

There is a way forward into God's best for our lives. He is the answer and He has the key. The story of the geese tells me that it is only too easy to become comfortable with far less than God intends for us. Please, please refuse to accept that, for God's sake as well as your own.

Psalm 84 teaches that, if it is in your heart, you reach the city of divine fullness where a vital and continuing intimate love relationship with our precious Lord Jesus becomes the norm. That Psalm also shows that the path may lead through a valley of tears, but even that can turn to a place of blessing and refreshing. Glory!

Sacramento

WE WENT TO SACRAMENTO, CALIFORNIA for two reasons at the natural level. It was more or less on our route home from Europe, and we had received an intriguing phone call when we were somewhere in Maryland or Virginia. The call was from a woman who knew of us because she and her husband had been missionaries in South Africa. We had not met them, but had enjoyed contacts with her dad who was still in South Africa at that time. During the call we were told, "We only have the best speakers in the world come to our church—but we would be happy to have you speak in some of our smaller meetings."

The first time I spoke was in an adult Sunday-School class with as many folk in attendance as some smaller church groups have in their services. That morning I smilingly asked them a provocative question, simply to have them focus on an area I had felt to challenge them about.

"You people say that you are baptized in the Holy Spirit, don't you?" I inquired. They agreed with that, so then came this outlandish question, "When you were baptized in the Spirit, did you get the big baptism or the little one?"

That certainly gained their somewhat bewildered attention! "No" I explained, "This isn't some new teaching or doctrine." I simply wanted to observe that people have all kinds of experiences with only a temporary and passing effect, when surely the Lord wants to develop an increasingly Christ-like character in every one of us. Some believers are baptized in the Spirit but, like coming out of a pool, soon dry off and are much the same as they were before. For others life is never the same again because it is lived on a higher plane from that day forward.

From then on I was approached by one person after another, each one asking how they could experience that life on a higher plane. I might also add as an aside that the pastor did actually ask me to share in a main church service before I left.

I sometimes wonder if it would make a difference to people's perceptions and understanding if we talked about being immersed in God rather than baptized in the Holy Spirit. Would it make a difference if we spoke of being filled with Christ, so that we are able to testify in very truth, "I live, but I don't live any longer. Christ lives in me." Although the other terminology is fully biblical, yet some interpretations, false emphases, and spurious experiences have given a wrong impression to many believers. Surely there can be no doubt that our wonderful heavenly Father has seen to it that full provision is made for each one of us to live triumphant, God-glorifying lives. God only gives good gifts.

Standing Tall

URING OUR STAY IN SACRAMENTO we were taken to see some of California's giant redwood trees. Some of these trees live up to 2,000 years though their average age is 500–700 years. Our friends drove us on a road that went right through a giant redwood tree. Yes, that's right. I understand that there are three such drive-through trees. Redwoods grow to over 120 metres [over 360 feet] so they really do stand tall! They are huge and quite majestic.

We came to a place where there was a large circle of these giant trees, and were given an explanation for them being like that. They were the 'offspring' of a tree that had been in the centre, but had long since died so that there was scarcely any sign of it remaining.

Seeing those trees, and thinking about them later, brought me to an interesting decision. I was audacious enough to choose to trust God, that by the grace of God, I could so live in Christ that over the coming years other believers would grow straight and true and 'stand tall.' This could result in their being a positive influence 'for good and for God' even when I was long since gone and forgotten.

Some of the things that can be passed on from one generation to another cannot be imparted in a short span of time. Seeing a younger generation walking steadfastly in the true humility of an intimate love relationship with the Lord Jesus is tremendously worthwhile.

Kingston, New York

W E HAVE VISITED SEVERAL FELLOW-
ships in the Kingston, New York area on
numerous occasions and have enjoyed
ready acceptance and sweet fellowship. Initially
we went at the invitation of Don Rumble whom we
had met in both Durban and Cape Town. On our
first visit to Kingston we stayed in the home of his
parents, Dale and Bertha Rumble, and immediately
felt a kinship in the Lord. I thoroughly enjoyed the
opportunity of input into the leadership, as well as of
ministering to the entire body there. On other visits
when we were more involved with their sister group
in Saugerties we enjoyed the warm hospitality of
John and Betty Whritenor.

Twice while we were in Kingston-Saugerties we
were given the opportunity of sharing on "My Father's Table," a programme aired on a local Christian
radio station. I found the second time particularly enjoyable as I was able to share from the freshness of
new things Father was showing me, and also some
of the good things that were being experienced in
our home fellowship in New Zealand. Resulting from

255

that we had worthwhile chats with people who attended meetings I was speaking at in the area.

I remember the day when someone asked me if I had been home for the weekend. I simply replied that I was from New Zealand, but they repeated their question. It would have taken us about 20 hours flying time each way to do that!

It reminds me of a day we were having lunch at a small restaurant in Boston, Mass. The waitress misheard what Mary ordered, and brought something else. After a while the waitress said very slowly and distinctly, "You—are—doing—good. You —speak— English—very—good." Since we were older than she was, we had been speaking the language longer, though of course with a different accent!

In my retirement in New Zealand I ride a mobility scooter. Once or twice someone has spoken like that to me here! I rode the scooter into a bakery and bought a couple of scones [translation: biscuits, in America]. The price tag said $1.10, so I gave the lady $2.20. She said, "Very—good! You—have—done— well. You—must—have—done—this—before." A bit pathetic I suppose, but quite laughable!

Bristol, Connecticut

W E FIRST CAME TO BRISTOL FROM New York where I had spoken to a group in Manhattan. It was agreed that we would drive up there after an evening service in Manhattan, obviously arriving very late. However, we were so late getting away from New York that our host there agreed to phone the Bristol folk and tell them we would arrive in the morning. We set out, but stopped at a motel on the way. When we reached there the next morning we discovered that they had not received a phone call and so had waited up for us until very late. Not a good way to be introduced to new people!

However, Gary and Linda Mears and Joe and Marion Dietrich were gracious and friendly. We came to love these folk and enjoy their company so much that there was a real tug at our hearts when it was suggested that we consider moving there permanently. However, we knew that such a thing was not for us. It was a privilege to have some involvement in their lives and in the developing life of the group of believers there.

One evening the elders met together and I was

with them. Initially I simply sat back listening to them discussing matters of local concern. After some time I felt that they were getting 'bogged down' a bit, so asked and received permission to put a question to them. "What would happen to the fellowship you feel such heavy responsibility for," I asked, "If God in His wisdom were to take all of you to heaven right now?"

After a few moments one of them caught my point, said so, and then joined the others in laughing at themselves. After all, the Lord Jesus said that He would build His church, and build it His way. I can almost hear Him saying, "It will be My way, or no way!" He is the Head.

Odessa, Texas

THE FLIGHT FROM NEW ZEALAND TO THE West Coast of the USA takes about twelve hours. It used to taken several hours longer when there were no direct flights and we flew into Hawaii first, usually having to go through immigration and custom checks there in the middle of the night. When we arrived in Los Angeles after such a flight I tried to phone Juan Carlos Ortiz. His wife told me that he was in Odessa, Texas and so we tried to arrange flights so that we could meet him there. There were very long queues at the airport and very long delays because DC 10 planes had been grounded all around the world.

Eventually we arrived in Odessa where I discussed with brother Ortiz details of his coming visit to New Zealand, for which I had undertaken to handle the arrangements. We enjoyed getting to know a number of pastors and other Christians in Odessa—Midland, resulting in our return to share in further meetings.

Maryland

WE MET LARRY AND PEGGY SMITH soon after our first arrival in Maryland. We have spent many happy days in their home at various times, and have often spoken at the Grace of God Fellowship in Glen Burnie, where Larry is the pastor. We have always been warmly welcomed and accepted. I recall a younger man in his congregation telling me that my preaching didn't do much for him, but he knew that Larry gained wonderful encouragement from my visits, and that was enough for him. Delightful honesty!

We have often stayed with Ed and Nancy Savich, and continue to maintain contact with them. We've shared many a conversation and many a laugh with these kind and hospitable friends, and with their sons Michael and Jeff as well. They took us to speak at the New Hope Baptist Church not far from their home.

It may have become the "old hope" because a few years later it ceased to exist! Once when I spoke there I couldn't help noticing a tall man sitting well to the back. He seemed to be so alive, and warmly responsive to what was shared. We had a nice chat together afterwards.

Much later, the elder of a Fellowship in New York State spoke to me about that man. I was told that he had missed the track, failed morally and been put under discipline by a trans-local group of church leaders. He was put out of ministry and told to go and submit to some brothers down in Florida, I think, which he apparently did. Those with oversight had instructed church people to have no contact with him.

That was all. Nothing else! I gave my observations to the elder, who had shared in the leadership group action. Any kind of discipline, no matter how justified, needs to have a redemptive factor to it. Surely every effort needs to be made to restore a man to a proper relationship with God, remembering 'There but for the grace of God, go I.'

Secondly, there surely must be some kind of plan to restore such a person to fellowship with other believers. No doubt a man like that needs to go through a new apprenticeship at the Lord's hands if he is ever to be restored to ministry—which is the sovereign choice of God, and may never happen. Twice, much later on, I spoke in a thriving gathering of believers in the Washington DC area that had been begun and was being led by that pastor.

On one occasion Ed and Nancy took me to a Restaurant in a Washington DC suburb where I was booked to speak at a Full Gospel Businessmen's Fellowship meeting. People facing the front didn't notice, but at one stage several sheriff's cars swooped up to the entrance of the meeting venue. Everyone had been singing songs of loving worship, with many raising their hands to the Lord. A passer-by had reported a hold up!

We met many delightful people at an Assembly in Clinton, Maryland. One Sunday morning I spoke to an old man I hadn't seen before. It was a simple word that I felt to pass on to him from the Lord, "Nothing is wasted. In spite of what may seem to have been wasted years, Father can use it all for His purposes."

The dear man wept and rejoiced. I had not known that he had been a preacher in his younger days, but had slipped away from God's best for his life. Doesn't the Lord promise to make up for the years the locusts have eaten?

Virginia

WE HAVE DELIGHTFUL MEMORIES OF our many visits to Richmond, Virginia. We have met a lot of lovely believers there being more involved with Bill Angus and Warren Weaver than anyone else. Four or five years ago I spent a little time in the USA on my way to Ireland, England, Zimbabwe and South Africa.

My only desire was to see Bill Angus for a few days, and go up to Charlottesville VA for a couple of days with Rudy and Pat Ramsey. Pat is in heaven now. While I was in Richmond John and Carol Milhous drove down from Amherst so that we could share a little time together. Over the years we have met these beloved friends in meetings and retreats, as well as been in their home.

I also had opportunity to have a meal at my motel near the Baltimore Washington International Airport with Larry and Peggy Smith and Ed and Nancy Savich. I believe that without exception all of us in that week or two were deeply aware of the Lord's presence with us as we shared spiritual things together. I briefly shared with all these good friends a message in word and song that I had received from the Lord to take to the saints in Dublin.

Some years ago when I had to undergo surgery in Richmond. Rudy and Pat told us later that we went through that entire experience for their sakes. It meant that we had opportunity through our rear-ranged schedule to spend a little time with them, which turned out to be of life-changing value. How good God is! Here is a copy of a letter Rudy wrote to us in February 2000:

"Pat and I both like to share with others that the Lord intervened in your life in Richmond, Virginia, and literally altered your agenda—itinerary—to bring you into our lives and to alter our course. The Lord has been faithful to keep us on track and has been kind enough to uproot some folks and bring them into our area to speed us on the way. Praise God! He used you to pretty much derail us [from our stifling old routine] and, through several of your books, to give us further direction.

"Truly, as you both well know, "All things do work together for our good" when we "love the Lord." I know it was no pleasure being sick and hospitalised, but the Lord used that in your life to bring you more

264

fully across my path when I was floundering and in need of direction.

"Your life ministered to us directly in answer to a prayer I prayed in January of 1990, "Lord, show me the church in your heart." In answer to that prayer, which I know came from Him, my life was turned upside down. In the midst of the upheaval he sent you and ministered through you to our needs at that time.

"Pat and I both want you to know how greatly we praise God for allowing you into our lives, and that we love you and greatly cherish that all too brief time we were allowed to fellowship with the two of you."

While referring to my illness in Richmond VA I must mention that Bill Angus was kindness itself to Mary and me during that testing time. We love Bill dearly. He has always shown a deep heart of love for the Lord as well as being loving and kind to us.

Here is something Bill Angus has shared about our involvement in his life:

"I remember meeting John Beaumont for the first time at a Full Gospel Businessmen's Meeting in Richmond, Virginia. John was different from most speakers we had heard. I had the impression that he was a

man who could hear God clearly and who ministered by direction from the Spirit of God in a new and fresh way. After that meeting I felt God prompting me to get to know John. He was very gracious to spend so much time with me. I had such a thirst for the things of God which he so freely ministered. This was the start of many years of friendship.

"I always felt like John was my spiritual mentor, giving me life long principles in following and listening to God to direct my life. John has written about his trip to California where he saw the redwood forest. There is a circle of offspring redwood trees around where the parent tree had been. I am one of those offspring redwood trees with a desire to follow the Lord in whatever way God directs. I want to say with all sincerity and love that by the grace of God this good friend of mine has been a great blessing and strength to me."

Destiny Image

MEETING DON AND KATHY NORI of Destiny Image was very meaningful to us. Without Don's encouragement and assistance I well may have never written one book. Realising that so many books are published these days, one has to wonder about it sometimes, yet I am grateful for many folk who have let us know that our writing has been meaningful to them, one way or another.

I am convinced that a ministry of encouragement is vitally necessary everywhere, and feel it is a privilege to encourage believers to see their walk with the Lord Jesus as an adventure of exploration into continuing freshness and newness.

America the Beautiful

WE HAVE SEEN SOME BEAUTIFUL scenery in the USA. To see the changing colour of trees in various States in the fall [autumn to us] has been very special. A day in Disney World in Florida was refreshing, although tiring at the same time. We have never seen ourselves as tourists and yet feel very privileged to have received the many 'extras' Father has provided. We thoroughly enjoyed our visits to Natural Bridge in Virginia.

I have been a traveller by the Lord's choice alone and yet I look back over the years with gratitude and praise for all the ways He has blessed and used us. The credit is all His for whatever has been accomplished.

Part 7

Retirement

O N OUR LAST VISIT TOGETHER TO THE United States of America, there were three occasions when someone approached me to share something they believed they were hearing from God, that affected me. At times I have felt that this kind of thing is one of the hazards of a travelling ministry!

Mary enjoys telling people of a man in South Africa prophesying [so he thought!] that God urgently wanted me to visit Namibia. My reply was "Father and I do not have a communication problem, so I will be sensitive to Him on the matter and respond to the Holy Spirit whenever He passes on further instructions." I never went to Namibia!

Now three different people unknown to each other, and in three different cities, had spoken to me, virtually with one voice. At least one of those men I had never met before, and the others I cannot remember anyway. Their message was that I could now return to enjoy the leisure of retirement at home in New Zealand. God had in hand the continuation of the things He had given me to share around the world, and assured me of a full harvest from the seed that had been sown. A great delight indeed!

After considering these matters before the Lord I

came to an assurance that this was the revelation of Father's present purpose for me. Because I was far from well at the time, I was especially grateful that I wasn't being set aside because of that, but rather because of a God appointed end to that phase of my life.

We were able to enjoy several years in a home Father provided for us at Diamond Harbour, where Mary's life-long wish to live overlooking a body of water was fulfiled. From there we moved into a flat [apartment] in the city of Christchurch where we obtained a delightful Cavalier King Charles spaniel. "Bolger" became an inseparable companion until dying of cancer at five years of age.

The neighbour in the adjoining flat decided to install a security system, and sent the salesperson in to see us. I had no interest in having such a system, and neither did Mary. However, I asked her, "If I went to heaven next week, would you be glad that it had been installed?" She replied, "No. I would immediately make plans to move into a retirement village."

Some weeks later I asked Mary if she was settled in her mind about the retirement village idea, and when she told me she was, I suggested we might as well look for such a place there and then, rather than leaving her to cope with it alone later.

We asked a Christian Realtor to give us a realistic appraisal of the value of our unit, because that would show us the limit available for purchasing a retirement village unit. I made clear that we were not putting the house on the market immediately, but would give him a sole agency if and when we did.

A week or two later Mary was swimming in a heated pool at a nearby indoor facility and the realtor swam over to her. She had never seen him swimming there before. He told her that he had no desire to pressure us, but wanted us to know that he had a cash buyer for our place if we were interested.

After Mary and I discussed this we decided to proceed. I set the price we would accept, although the agent thought it was on the high side. It was sold in a matter of days for our asking price. By then we had checked out quite a number of retirement villages, narrowing our choice down to three before making a final decision.

That night, without my knowledge, Mary prayed

[in a way I would not!] that the Lord would close the door to two of the three places. Next morning she rang the three, and only one had a unit available. And so we came to the Linrose Retirement Village, and are enjoyably satisfied and totally contented here.

After being here a year I wrote a leaflet about the lifestyle available in a place like this. Mary had urged me to do so because there was too much adverse publicity and inaccurate information about retirement villages being spread around the city.

By then I had started going to the Friday night 'Happy Hours' in the village community centre, even though I do not drink alcohol. I detest it! I had felt by the persuasion of the Holy Spirit that a Pharisee wouldn't go, but Jesus would. Oops!

One night about half a dozen men at the table where I sat asked about the brochure and inquired whether I had written anything else. I told them I had and answered, "This and that" when they wanted to know what I wrote about. One of the men asked, "You write spiritual?" I told them that my writing centred on the Lord Jesus. For the rest of the hour those guys fired questions at me. Discussion centred on salvation through faith in the Lord Jesus and the reality of heaven. One of the men asked several times, "But we have to make a choice, don't we John?"

Because quite a number of us were hard of hearing we were all speaking quite loudly. Mary heard us at her table and told me that others were also listening. At the end I told the guys that I believed in God, believed in prayer and believed in salvation. I would always be available for personal conversation.

Prior to a village dinner and social evening in the Retirement Village we all talked about 'standing tall'. Mary and I interviewed everyone who wished to participate, asking them about special memories, remarkable events, things they were proud of, weird, wonderful or hilarious incidents, major decisions, and so forth.

Quite a number told us of their disillusionment with 'the church'. I told them that God and the church are very different, since the church they spoke of is man-made and man-controlled. None of them denied that.

My cousin Roy Simons, who lived here, shared a glowing testimony of the difference Christ had made in his life. A week or two later he died suddenly at the ripe old age of eighty-five. I printed out the things he had shared with us, which included comments about family life and his receiving an award for bravery in the second world war, and provided a copy to each resident in the village.

To my surprise, one of the things Mary wrote for distribution in the village was that she was proud of my ordination. There is a line to a hymn in the Keswick hymnbook that was used when we were young, "Mine the mighty ordination of the nail-pierced hands." That is the only ordination I feel comfortable with.

I jokingly asked Mary, "Is that all you are proud about in my life?" Her reply is quite humbling to me except that it obviously magnifies the grace of God. Because of that it is fitting to end this narrative with what she wrote. Here it is:

"Things I am proud of in my husband John:

"1. His undivided devotion to God even in the midst of weakness and personal suffering, truly denying self, taking up his cross daily and gladly, to serve his Master.

"2. His giving spirit to all in need—a generosity of heart.

"3. His ability to relate to leaders of all races. His dealing with problems and failure, where necessary, without fear or favour and with a redemptive quality. His lovingly coming alongside a brother in ministry.

"4. Finding the 'mind of God' when ministering rather than dishing out 'old hat'.

"5. Doing his utmost to be a good father. Having time for his boys to take them on picnics and outings when they were little. To this day he is available to them and willing to give time, interest and support whenever he can assist them.

"6. Overcoming natural desires, e.g. to be a hermit, to relate to others and be an available man.

"7. To love me unconditionally in spite of many annoying traits, and be willing to help and comfort me when really needing this more himself."

In all honesty I must point out that Mary's pure heart of love for her Lord, and her sweet caring spirit, results in far fewer 'annoying traits' than her husband has!

Let me conclude with a restatement of a Bible verse that was vital to me in my youth, that has been a principle in my life over the years, and still means a great deal to me today. Here it is paraphrased:

"Not by human strength or ability, nor by the supportive power of an army of men, but by my Spirit says the Lord of heaven's armies."

Farewell.

John Beaumont—In Christ, where grace ALWAYS abounds!

RECOMMENDED READING

CUSTOM AND COMMAND

STAN FIRTH, WHO WROTE THE FOREWORD to *A God-Filled Nobody* has written a delightful and inspiring book, *Custom and Command*, which he distributes personally. Many believers around the world have found both comfort and challenge through this book.

Custom and Command brings encouragement from the Scriptures to a new breed of Christians—with some answers to those who might feel critical of them.

It is available from:

> Mr J. S. Firth,
> c/o 2c, Gander Green Lane,
> SUTTON, Surrey,
> SM1 2EH,
> England.
> e-mail: stanfirth@ukonline.co.uk